## DATE DUE

|  |  |  |  |
|---|---|---|---|
|  |  |  |  |
|  |  |  |  |
|  |  |  |  |
|  |  |  |  |
|  |  |  |  |
|  |  |  |  |
|  |  |  |  |
|  |  |  |  |
|  |  |  |  |
|  |  |  |  |
|  |  |  |  |
|  |  |  |  |
|  |  |  |  |
|  |  |  |  |
|  |  |  |  |
|  |  |  |  |
|  |  |  |  |
|  |  |  |  |

DEMCO 38-297

# JAMES WELCH

**Critical Companions to Popular Contemporary Writers**
**Second Series**

Isabel Allende *by Karen Castellucci Cox*

Julia Alvarez *by Silvio Sirias*

Rudolfo A. Anaya *by Margarite Fernandez Olmos*

Maya Angelou *by Mary Jane Lupton*

Ray Bradbury *by Robin Anne Reid*

Revisiting Mary Higgins Clark *by Linda De Roche*

Louise Erdrich *by Lorena L. Stookey*

Ernest J. Gaines *by Karen Carmean*

Gabriel García Márquez *by Rubén Pelayo*

Kaye Gibbons *by Mary Jean DeMarr*

John Irving *by Josie P. Campbell*

Garrison Keillor *by Marcia Songer*

Jamaica Kincaid *by Lizabeth Paravisini-Gebert*

Revisiting Stephen King *by Sharon A. Russell*

Barbara Kingsolver *by Mary Jean DeMarr*

Maxine Hong Kingston *by E. D. Huntley*

Terry McMillan *by Paulette Richards*

Larry McMurtry *by John M. Reilly*

Toni Morrison *by Missy Dehn Kubitschek*

Walter Mosley *by Charles E. Wilson, Jr.*

Gloria Naylor *by Charles E. Wilson, Jr.*

James Patterson *by Joan G. Kotker*

Chaim Potok *by Sanford Sternlicht*

Amy Tan *by E. D. Huntley*

Anne Tyler *by Paul Bail*

Leon Uris *by Kathleen Shine Cain*

Kurt Vonnegut *by Thomas F. Marvin*

Tom Wolfe *by Brian Abel Ragen*

# JAMES WELCH

## *A Critical Companion*

### Mary Jane Lupton

CRITICAL COMPANIONS TO POPULAR CONTEMPORARY WRITERS
Kathleen Gregory Klein, Series Editor

**Greenwood Press**
**Westport, Connecticut • London**

**Library of Congress Cataloging-in-Publication Data**

Lupton, Mary Jane.
    James Welch : a critical companion / Mary Jane Lupton.
       p.  cm. — (Critical companions to popular contemporary writers, ISSN 1082–4979)
    Includes bibliographical references and index.
    ISBN: 0–313–32725–4
       1. Welch, James, 1940—Criticism and interpretation—Handbooks,
    manuals, etc.  2. Western stories—History and criticism—Handbooks,
    manuals, etc.  3. West (U.S.)—In literature—Handbooks, manuals, etc.  4.
    Indians in literature—Handbooks, manuals, etc.  I. Title.  II. Series.
    PS3573.E44Z76  2004
    813'.54—dc22       2004000180

British Library Cataloguing in Publication Data is available.

Library of Congress Catalog Card Number: 2004000180
ISBN: 0–313–32725–4
ISSN: 1082–4979

First published in 2004

Greenwood Press, 88 Post Road West, Westport, CT 06881
An imprint of Greenwood Publishing Group, Inc.
www.greenwood.com

Printed in the United States of America

The paper used in this book complies with the
Permanent Paper Standard issued by the National
Information Standards Organization (Z39.48–1984).

10  9  8  7  6  5  4  3  2  1

In Memory of James Welch (1940–2003)

# Contents

# Series Foreword

The authors who appear in the series Critical Companions to Popular Contemporary Writers are all best-selling writers. They do not simply have one successful novel, but a string of them. Fans, critics, and specialist readers eagerly anticipate their next book. For some, high cash advances and breakthrough sales figures are automatic; movie deals often follow. Some writers become household names, recognized by almost everyone.

But, their novels are read one by one. Each reader chooses to start and, more importantly, to finish a book because of what she or he finds there. The real test of a novel is in the satisfaction its readers experience. This series acknowledges the extraordinary involvement of readers and writers in creating a best-seller.

The authors included in this series were chosen by an Advisory Board composed of high school English teachers and high school and public librarians. They ranked a list of best-selling writers according to their popularity among different groups of readers. For the first series, writers in the top-ranked group who had received no book-length, academic, literary analysis (or none in at least the past ten years) were chosen. Because of this selection method, Critical Companions to Popular Contemporary Writers meets a need that is being addressed nowhere else. The success of these volumes as reported by reviewers, librarians, and teachers led to an expansion of the series mandate to include some writers with wide critical attention—Toni Morrison, John Irving, and Maya Angelou, for example—to extend the usefulness of the series.

The volumes in the series are written by scholars with particular expertise in analyzing popular fiction. These specialists add an academic focus to the popular success that these writers already enjoy.

The series is designed to appeal to a wide range of readers. The general reading public will find explanations for the appeal of these well-known writers. Fans will find biographical and fictional questions answered. Students will find literary analysis, discussions of fictional genres, carefully organized introductions to new ways of reading the novels, and bibliographies for additional research. Whether browsing through the book for pleasure or using it for an assignment, readers will find that the most recent novels of the authors are included.

Each volume begins with a biographical chapter drawing on published information, autobiographies or memoirs, prior interviews, and, in some cases, interviews given especially for this series. A chapter on literary history and genres describes how the author's work fits into a larger literary context. The following chapters analyze the writer's most important, most popular, and most recent novels in detail. Each chapter focuses on one or more novels. This approach, suggested by the Advisory Board as the most useful to student research, allows for an in-depth analysis of the writer's fiction. Close and careful readings with numerous examples show readers exactly how the novels work. These chapters are organized around three central elements: plot development (how the story line moves forward), character development (what the reader knows of the important figures), and theme (the significant ideas of the novel). Chapters may also include sections on generic conventions (how the novel is similar or different from others in its same category of science fiction, fantasy, thriller, etc.), narrative point of view (who tells the story and how), symbols and literary language, and historical or social context. Each chapter ends with an "alternative reading" of the novel. The volume concludes with a primary and secondary bibliography, including reviews.

The alternative readings are a unique feature of this series. By demonstrating a particular way of reading each novel, they provide a clear example of how a specific perspective can reveal important aspects of the book. In the alternative reading sections, one contemporary literary theory—way of reading, such as feminist criticism, Marxism, new historicism, deconstruction, or Jungian psychological critique—is defined in brief, easily comprehensible language. That definition is then applied to the novel to highlight specific features that might go unnoticed or be understood differently in a more general reading. Each volume defines two or three specific theories, making them part of the reader's understanding of how diverse meanings may be constructed from a single novel.

Taken collectively, the volumes in the Critical Companions to Popular Contemporary Writers series provide a wide-ranging investigation of the complexities of current best-selling fiction. By treating these novels seriously as both literary works and publishing successes, the series demonstrates the potential of popular literature in contemporary culture.

Kathleen Gregory Klein
Southern Connecticut State University

# Acknowledgments

My first debt of gratitude is to my husband Kenneth Huntress Baldwin (Ken) for library books procured, ink ribbons replaced, scholarly essays photocopied, and a personal computer available for instant use whether I was writing in Cape May, New Jersey, or in Baltimore, Maryland. I thank him for assisting in the interview with Jim and Lois Welch in July 2002, and then for driving the two of us to the North American Indian Days powwow in Browning, Montana, where Welch was born and where Ken and I had a transcendent cultural experience on the Indian side of Glacier National Park. Above all, I thank Ken for the tolerance and love he showed me during this project, particularly when I was distressed.

Jim and Lois Welch were very gracious in extending an interview to my husband and me at their home in Missoula, Montana, in July 2002. I am grateful to Jim Welch for having granted me not one but two interviews, the first in Baltimore in November 2001. These interviews have helped me to understand his complexity, both as a novelist and as a person.

I am also grateful to my friend since 1970, Aimee Wiest, who kindly loaned me her personal library on Native American culture and who was able to retrieve *Medicine Cards: The Discovery of Power Through the Way of Animals* from her cluttered attic so that I could fathom the magic of the raven and the grizzly.

Many of my colleagues at Morgan State University assisted me with encouragement and information during the earliest stages of this project.

I thank President Earl Richardson for granting me the status of Professor Emeritus and for continuing to invite me to commencement and to other major university functions. Other Morgan colleagues who earn my specific thanks are Jewel Chambers, for giving me a prepublication copy of Larry Colton's novel *Counting Coup;* Caleb Corkery, for filling in my gaps on the topics of Indians and basketball; Milford Jeremiah, for having given me news clippings on Native Americans; and my friend Caroline Maun—for her technical advice, her wet-weather photographing of the arrival of the Len'ape Indians at Cape May Point in September 2002, and her love.

I thank the many graduate students in the MA program at Morgan State University, whom I taught for 30 years, for keeping me alert as I made the transitions from psychoanalytic criticism to feminist criticism to African American Studies to Native American Studies. My special thanks go to Suzanne Beale, Maria Boston, Jane Donovan, Linda Myers, Ella Stevens, and Aimee Wiest; and above all to Leslie Person, the graduate student who, six years ago, insisted, against my better judgment, that she do her research project on a book I'd never heard of—James Welch's *Fools Crow.*

I am grateful to Felicia Campbell of the Far West Popular Culture Association for accepting two of my conference papers on James Welch, in 1999 and 2000, papers that were my initiation into this longer project.

I also want to thank the following people for their information, their telephone calls, their e-mails, and their general encouragement: Tom Crane, Linda Fool Bear, Joyce Ford, Chief Mark Gould and his wife (Delaware/ Len'ape), Janice Klein, Elaine Markson, Medicine Warrior (Cherokee), Kathleen L. Nichols, Jane Roop (Cherokee), Donelle Ruwe, Greg Salyer, Nina Tassi, Elizabeth Watson, and Lois Welch. I truly apologize for any omissions.

I owe a special debt to Jack and Carol Ann Hohman, my brother and sister-in-law, for representing the family at my retirement banquet on May 5, 1991, and for helping me play bridge under a more advanced bidding system than the one that our dear parents, Ruth and George Hohman, taught us 50 years ago in Pottsville, Pennsylvania. I thank my twin daughters, Ellen Lupton and Julia Lupton, for the many gifts they have given me over the years—a trip to the California wine country; a trip to Barcelona; an emergency medical consultation; a first edition of William Farr's *The Reservation Blackfeet;* two liberal, sensitive sons-in-law; six phenomenal grandchildren; and themselves.

I would like to thank my editor at Greenwood Press, Lynn Araujo, whose immediate answers to my e-mail queries regarding form, punctuation, and fair use helped facilitate the writing of the rough draft. I am especially grateful for her wise suggestions for revision. Finally, I would like to thank Marilyn Stone for her meticulous copyediting of the manuscript.

# 1

# Biographical Background on James Welch: Poet and Novelist

James Welch, Blackfeet novelist and poet (1940–2003), was one of the first contemporary Indian writers to introduce the Native voice into American literature. A lone wolf, Welch was writing poetry in 1966, before there was an established body of written literature that could be grouped under what is currently called the Native American Renaissance. "As far as I knew back then, there were no Indian writers. . . . Now you don't shake a tree without two or three Indian writers falling out" (Introduction, *Third Catalog of Native American Literature* 1997, 2). This droll comment on Indian heritage is rather typical of James Welch, who had a humorous sense of self-assessment, especially when he engaged, as "Jim," in an informal essay or an interview.

Generally, though, James Welch was serious. As an Indian writer he looked to his Blackfeet past, discovering both meaning and identity in the culture of northwestern Montana. "It's becoming more and more acceptable to say *Indians*. Those days of pain and so on are fading. People on reservations call each other Indians" ("Baltimore Interview"). Like him, I use the culturally identified term *Indian* throughout this book unless the more academic phrase "Native American" seems more appropriate. This book will demonstrate Welch's importance in the formation of an Indian and an American narrative tradition. He will be compared with other

Indian, European, and American writers and filmmakers who, like him, have stimulated their audiences with stories of frustration, sacrifice, and celebration.

In his fiction Welch gave a diverse account of Indian life in America from multiple perspectives: a nameless cattle rancher (*Winter in the Blood*, 1974); an alcoholic half-breed (*The Death of Jim Loney*, 1979); a nineteenth-century Plains warrior *(Fools Crow,* 1986); a successful Indian politician (*The Indian Lawyer*, 1991); an Oglala Sioux abandoned in Southern France (*The Heartsong of Charging Elk,* 2000). Welch never told the same story.

General information about Welch's life and achievements has been presented in numerous interviews, reviews, and articles. I have relied on general material in reconstructing such matters as awards, public speaking, and professional development. Specific acknowledgment is given when the information is distinctive to a particular source or to a particular historical or cultural event. Both kinds of information have been grouped in the bibliography under the heading "Biographical Sources."

## INTERVIEWING WELCH

I first met James Welch in November 2001, having arranged an interview with him while he was in Baltimore at the annual convention of the National Council of Teachers of English. Welch was a featured NCTE speaker. A slight man of mixed heritage, he was immediately recognizable because I had watched the video he made for the Native American Humanities Series several times in anticipation of our meeting. "People get upset because I don't look like an Indian," he had confessed (*Native American Novelists Series* 1999). Accompanying James Welch was his non-Indian wife, Lois, a retired professor of Comparative Literature at the University of Montana. I promised to end the interview in an hour so that the Welches would have time for lunch before Welch's keynote address. It was an exciting hour that focused on Welch's literary works. I call this the "Baltimore Interview."

Eight months later my husband, Ken Baldwin, and I met James and Lois Welch in their own territory at their home in Missoula, Montana, several days before Ken and I attended the Native American Indian Days Celebration held annually in Browning, where Welch was born. I refer to the second meeting as the "Montana Interview." I draw upon each meeting extensively throughout this book to support biographical, literary, and cultural information.

James Phillip Welch lived in Missoula with his wife, the former Lois

Monk. They were married in 1968 and eventually bought a charming farm house on Rattlesnake Creek on the outskirts of Missoula. The house has a white fence and a grape arbor. When we were there, we were entertained by a golden retriever named Ned.

When I later asked Lois about Ned, she told me that he was the third golden retriever in the family. The second one, Bill, was a mischievous dog who one day chewed up Jim's notes to *Fools Crow*. Fortunately, Lois was able to tape the notes together and iron them into shape (phone conversation, 20 Nov. 2003).

Near the doorbell I noticed a small sign that said, "Only one chief lives here," a sign that from a feminist perspective suggests that only one of the Welches is the boss or "chief," as in the old "bossy spouse" jokes.

"The sign is just a joke instead of a statement," Jim Welch insisted.

"I see it's twice as much a joke. It is a joke," Lois agreed.

## ANCESTRY

Welch was born in 1940 in the hospital on the Blackfeet reservation in Browning, Montana. His mother was a member of the Gros Ventre tribe and his father was a Blackfeet. His grandfathers were Irish. His father taught him about his ancestors and took the family on visits to other Indian reservations, including one stay in Alaska (*Native American Novelists Series* 1999). It was on a visit to an encampment near Two Medicine River near Browning where Welch first witnessed the sacred ceremony of the Sun Dance. As the elders entered the medicine lodge, "a voice, high and distant, sang to the sun and it entered my bones and I was Blackfeet and changed forever" (Foreword, Farr 1984, viii).

Welch was proud of his Indian heritage. "I have always considered myself an Indian," he stated in a taped interview. As a child he would roam the hills outside Browning with his Indian friends. It was a "fairly idyllic place to grow up" (*Native American Novelists Series* 1999). When he was at his mother's Fort Belknap reservation, Welch recalls having watched cowboy and Indian movies with the Gros Ventre children. He remarked that he found himself rooting for John Wayne (*Native American Novelists Series* 1999). Although as a child he was raised in the Catholic faith, he later saw himself as an agnostic, someone who cannot know if there is a Divine Power. "I do believe in the viability of spiritualism, however," he told Don Lee (Lee 1994, 197).

In an interview with Ron McFarland, Welch spoke fondly of his parents, who were hard workers and good providers. His father, who survives him, was at various times a welder, a hospital administrator, a rancher, and a farmer. His mother, Rosella O'Bryan, spent her childhood on the Fort Belknap reservation, leaving to attend Haskell Institute in Kansas for a secretarial program. As a stenographer she proffered her skills to a number of reservations and community centers (McFarland 2000, 1–2). Welch also had two brothers, one a forester and the other a farmer ("Montana Interview").

The major source for Welch's stories was his grandmother, who in turn passed them on to his Blackfeet father. In addition, he learned about his ancestry by listening to the elders who sat in front of the grocery story in Browning, Montana (*Native American Novelists Series* 1999). These traditional stories have affected much of Welch's fiction and poetry, but most importantly *Fools Crow*. Thanks to the work of ethnographers George Bird Grinnell, Walter McClintock, Clark Wissler, D.C. Duvall, and other late nineteenth–/early twentieth–century preservers of Blackfeet culture, current readers are able to trace many of Welch's references to their original sources.

James Welch's great-grandmother was one of the survivors of the massacre at Marias Creek in Oklahoma territory in 1870; and one of his relatives, Malcolm Clark, was the white settler whose death may have caused the Marias massacre, in which more than 100 nonhostile Indian people were slaughtered. Another relative helped preserve Blackfeet history by developing a method for recording the deeds of elder warriors (McFarland 1986, 14–15).

When I asked Welch what was the preferred form—Blackfeet or Blackfoot—he told me, "I feel comfortable saying 'Blackfeet' because the people in Montana call themselves 'Blackfeet.' They are one of the three tribes of 'The Blackfeet Nation'—or the 'Blackfoot Nation.' Two of the tribes live up in Canada: the Bloods and the Siksika [who are called the Blackfoot]. The Pikuni are in Montana. Here we call them 'Blackfeet.' Every official thing that we get from the tribe is 'The Blackfeet'" ("Montana Interview"). Throughout this book I use the plural form.

Welch admitted that neither term is indigenous to the original people of the Northern Plains. But contemporary Indians have adopted the word *Blackfeet*, a settler name signifying ashes on their feet, because the old language is disappearing. "Now almost every young person speaks only English," he said. "And in my generation most of us speak only English. So we've kind of taken these words over into our English language." Welch himself speaks only English, although his father still speaks the old language ("Montana Interview").

The Gros Ventre, his mother's people, were once friendly with the Blackfeet but became hostile in the early 1860s (Lang 2002, par 1). Both his maternal and paternal grandfathers were Irish men who had married Indian women (*Native American Novelists Series* 1999). As William Farr and other historians have stated, mixed marriages were a common practice on the Blackfeet reservation in the nineteenth century (Farr 1984, 168).

Welch began his schooling on the Blackfeet and Belknap Reservations. According to Lois Welch, he attended junior high school in Pickstown, South Dakota. One of his classmates was Tom Brokaw, who later became one of America's leading newscasters (phone conversation, 20 Nov. 2003). The family then moved to Minneapolis, where Welch attended Lashburn High School. Here he developed an early interest in poetry. Welch confessed that he was embarrassed by his poetry and hid it from his classmates, fearing that they would label him a sissy (*Native American Novelists Series* 1999). After graduating from Lashburn High in 1958, he attended both the University of Minnesota and Northern Montana College before earning a Bachelor of Arts degree from the University of Montana at Missoula in 1965. He then joined the Writing Seminar at the University of Montana, never completing the MFA degree.

In describing his apprenticeship as a poet and novelist, Welch acknowledged his debt to Richard Hugo (1923–1982), who directed the Writing Seminar at the University of Montana. Welch said, "He was an amazing poet and an amazing teacher. He was an incredible influence on me. He made me realize that anyone could write poetry. I used to have these Romantic visions of 'The Poet.' He demystified poetry, and I think that was as important as anything else he could teach. He was a tremendous influence not only on me but on other poets, some of whom are still publishing today." Hugo's influence, though, had little effect on Indians other than Welch. "There weren't very many Indians writing," Welch said ("Baltimore Interview").

Those Indians who were working in the creative arts were gleaning their models, as did Welch, from a Euro-American tradition—from a literature dominated by white American male novelists like John Steinbeck and Ernest Hemingway and by European poets like William Shakespeare and John Keats, by what Welch had called "Romantic visions of 'The Poet.'" Welch was quick to admit his debt both to Ernest Hemingway and to a less common model, the Italian surrealist Elio Vittorini, whose *Conversations in Sicily* has a narrative technique similar to Welch's *Winter in the Blood* (Ruoff 1989, 151–57). But it was Richard Hugo who taught him that "you can wear blue jeans and T-shirts and still be a poet" ("Baltimore Interview").

Hugo, a poet from Seattle who had attended the University of Washington, was in the Army Air Corps in the Second World War and did several missions over Italy and Germany. He came back to the United States, finished his MA at the University of Washington, and on the strength of his writing was invited to teach writing at the University of Montana, where he remained until he died. Four years after Hugo's death, James and Lois Welch, along with Hugo's widow, Ripley, edited *The Real West Marginal Way*, a collection of Hugo's autobiographical essays.

Welch was perhaps even more uncertain with his early efforts at fiction than he was with his poetry.

> The first version [of *Winter in the Blood*] was really terrible," he told me. "I didn't know how to write a novel. So I showed it to Bill Kitteredge [who later would coedit an anthology of writings from Montana]. I showed him the first draft and he said, 'Why don't you come over tonight and we'll talk about it?'
>
> I had high hopes. But every single page was all marked up. And we went through that virtually page by page. He just tore through it, but in a good way. He tried to help me out. But it was so discouraging that I just put it in my bottom drawer. ("Montana Interview")

Welch didn't even tell his wife about it until they went to Greece. "I got it out of the drawer, took it along, just for kicks. And that's when I wrote the next three drafts" ("Montana Interview").

## CONTRIBUTIONS AND AWARDS

Welch's stature as a writer has been recognized by Indian readers as well as by scholars from predominantly white universities. After the publication of *The Heartsong of Charging Elk* in fall 2000, he became a perhaps unwilling spokesperson for Indian literature and culture. A highly selective survey of the Internet reveals his accelerated commitment to public speaking during the few years preceding his death.

In early November 2000 he was an invited speaker at Yale University. In September of 2001 he was keynote speaker at the Great Salt Lake Book Festival in Utah. On October 11, 2001, he was a panelist at the Free Library of Philadelphia, and on November 3, 2001, he spoke about *The Heartsong of Charging Elk* at the Chicago Humanities Festival. Two weeks later he was in Baltimore for the National Council of Teachers of English convention. In April 2002 he was a visiting author for the Minnesota Writers Conference. His various public appearances seem to diverge from what he told me during our meeting in Baltimore when I asked him if he lectured in schools and libraries. "Not so much," he answered. "In fact, in the last few years I've tried to cut back on traveling around" ("Baltimore Interview").

As effective as he may have been at public speaking, James Welch was foremost a writer, a careful artist who sometimes did three or four drafts of a single novel. His books have become required reading across the nation, from high school literature classes to graduate courses in Native American Studies at University of California, Los Angeles, and other major institutions. Advanced degree candidates are beginning to chose Welch as the subject of their doctoral research. His name appears in the subtitle of a dissertation written by Blanca Scorcht Chester (November 2000), and Welch told us that a doctoral candidate at the University of Montana has nearly completed her dissertation on his works. At the time of this writing there is only one book-length analysis of his novels: Ron McFarland's *Understanding James Welch*, published by the University of South Carolina Press in 2000, a year short of the appearance of Welch's fifth novel, *The Heartsong of Charging Elk*.

Welch's novels have earned him numerous awards. In 1997 he received a major tribute from the Indian community when he became the recipient of the Native Writer's Lifetime Achievement Award for his accomplishments in Indian fiction, poetry, and history.

Although some of his awards are regional, like the Pacific Bookseller's Association Book Awards in 2001, others have been national or international in scope. The French government applauded Welch's achievements by bestowing upon him the medal of the Chevalier de L'Ordre des Arts et des Lettres for his "outstanding service to French culture" (*Yale Bulletin and Calendar* 2000, 1). He became well enough established in the literary community to endorse fledgling Indian novelists like Debra Magpie Earling, whose novel *Perma Red* he described as "a startlingly spiritual novel of the lives and loves and heartbreak on a Montana Indian reservation" (Bantam Catalog 2003; see Earling 2003).

Having learned so much from Jim Welch during our interviews, I was hoping to speak with him one more time before this book went into production. He was scheduled to participate at an Institute on American Indian Art and Literature, sponsored by the National Endowment for the

Humanities, to be held in the summer of 2003. When I emailed for further details I was informed that Welch had canceled because he was not well. I later learned that Welch had been struggling against lung cancer. He died on Monday, August 4, 2003, at the age of 62, of a heart attack (*Salt Lake City Tribune* 2003).

## NATIVE AMERICAN STUDIES

The contributions of James Welch and other contemporary Native American writers go largely unrecognized. When Indian peoples and their individual cultures are acknowledged, it is frequently through a Euro-American filter.

In September 2002 I spoke with a Nanticoke/Lena'pe woman who had supported an entourage of canoes and kayaks that made a 330-mile journey from upper New York state to southern New Jersey. Their mission was twofold: to create an awareness of the need to stop pollution on the Delaware River and to identify the Lena'pe and other Eastern tribes as having been the first people to settle what we now call America. The woman, second wife of Chief Mark Gould, told me that she and her daughter had done a lot of educational programs. "The children, and it's no fault of theirs because we're not in the history books, think that all Indians live out west on reservations. We keep getting: 'Are you really Indian?' 'Do you live in a teepee?' 'Do you dress like that all of the time?'

"It's sad," she continued, "the ignorance that's still out there today. My daughter and I, when she was younger, did I bet to say 50 to 60 programs in a school year at different elementary schools, churches, boy scouts, just to make the awareness" (excerpt from Lupton, "Interview with Lena'pe Indians," 5 Sept. 2002).

The awareness Gould and others like her are advocating is bound to have an impact on general education programs in this country. College professors and editors of scholarly journals are applying similar pressure. The University of Nebraska has established two series devoted to Indian writers. One is "Contemporary Indigenous Issues," edited by Devon Abbott Mihesuah. This series will examine the decolonization of American Indian women, the rewriting on tribal history, and Indians in sports. A second series, edited by Gerald Vizenor and Diane Glancy, will publish "stories that express a Native American fictional consciousness" (Monaghan 2003, A16).

Another source of learning is being fostered within the Indian communities themselves, as the people seek a reintroduction to the language that was denied them in the federal government's plan to force students to attend schools off the reservation such as the Carlisle Indian Industrial School in Pennsylvania, founded in 1879. "Everyone at Carlisle had to speak English; on pain of corporal punishment, no tribal language was allowed without permission" (Woodhead 1995, 95).

In the past several decades there has been a strong movement to revitalize the Native languages and culture. Darrell Kipp and a few associates in Montana founded the Piegan Institute and in 1995 opened the Nizipuhwashin ("Real Speak") Center so that students of all ages could study the Blackfeet language. The institute uses an "immersion-school model" aimed at bringing back the language that had been so discouraged a century earlier. Similar schools have been founded in Nevada and Wisconsin (Nijhuis 2002, 11,16). Novelist N. Scott Momaday, in a statement advocating Indian self-identity, writes, "The greatest risk to Indian people in the 21st century is that of losing their fundamental knowledge of who they are and who they are supposed to be. Without that knowledge there comes the loss of will, of confidence, of the very self that is essential to all else" (Momaday 2002, 12).

Few non-Indians are aware of the primacy of the Indian nations. James Welch, one of the most widely recognized Indian writers of the late twentieth/early twenty-first century, is still underrepresented in high school and college reading lists, despite his increasing popularity. Among Welch's contemporaries this same underrepresentation occurs. References to other Indian writers are interjected throughout this book in order to place Welch within a current framework and to facilitate the readers' awareness of other Indian texts.

## AUTOBIOGRAPHICAL ELEMENTS IN *KILLING CUSTER*

In his autobiographical preface to William Farr's *The Reservation Blackfeet*, Welch describes an early memory of being an Indian. When he was nine years old his father took him to a plain south of Browning, where they saw painted tepees and old cars gathered in circles. Welch remembers: "The air smelled of smoky buckskin and sagebrush and the burning sweetgrass." He was witnessing his first Sun Dance ceremony. "Thirty-four years later the image of that Sun Dance procession is still with me, and in my novels and poems I have tried to maintain the spirit of that moment" (Farr 1984, vii).

James Welch has indeed maintained that spirit, not only in his poetry and fiction but also in *Killing Custer*, a remarkable piece of nonfiction that is his major contribution to the history of the American Indian. Long before John G. Neihardt first transcribed Black Elk's account of the Battle of Wounded Knee, there had been an orally documented record of the Plains Wars and of the confiscation of Indian lands. *Bury My Heart at Wounded Knee,* Dee Brown's 1970 expose of the settlers' brutality toward Indians, is still the most popular written history, although other books such as *These Barren Lands* by Paula Mitchell Marks (1998) and the classic *Custer Died for Your Sins* (Vine Deloria 1969) are only two of the many other historical studies of the settlers' destruction of this continent's original people. I am using *settlers* to indicate people of European descent who went west in search of land and gold, following the model established by Dee Horne in her book *Contemporary American Indian Writing* (1999).

*Killing Custer* is an unusual book, part history and part autobiography, part about making a film and part about Welch's personal involvement in researching the material. Here Welch presents the famous Battle of Little Bighorn (June 25, 1876) from the Indian side, basing much of his information on interviews conducted among Indians whose grandparents or other elders had won the decisive victory against the Seventh Cavalry in the fields of southeastern Montana. He surrounds the most notorious military figure of the century, General George Armstrong Custer, with known Sioux and Cheyenne warriors—surrounding him on the printed page much as Native Americans had once surrounded and annihilated the Seventh Cavalry. The title has a double meaning; it is about the death of Custer but it is also about Welch's approach. He is literally killing the Custer of Western myth by reconstructing history from an inside or indigenous perspective, with the narratives of Sitting Bull, Crazy Horse, and Red Cloud overshadowing the blond-haired soldier from West Point.

Sitting Bull, the head of the Hunkpapa Sioux and the chief of the gathering of more than 7,000 Indians camping on the banks of the Little Bighorn on the day of Custer's attack, receives Welch's greatest attention. Sitting Bull was spiritually prepared for the assault, for he had sliced his arms, removing 50 small pieces of skin from each. After his self-mutilation he had a dream vision in which he had seen soldiers falling from the sky "like grasshoppers, with their heads down and their hats off" (*Killing Custer* 1994, 51).

In various interviews Welch explained the genesis of *Killing Custer*. He had been doing research on the video *Last Stand at Little Bighorn* (1992). His editor suggested that he transform the research for the film into a book, one that would establish Indian supremacy in what history has labeled "Custer's Last Stand." "Actually, it started as a documentary film," Welch said. "I had never written nonfiction before. It was hard. It was very difficult. I didn't know what tone to take. I didn't know how personal one could get with nonfiction" ("Baltimore Interview").

Welch gets very personal in *Killing Custer,* giving the historical exploration an autobiographical emphasis that exists side-by-side with his dedication to Indian history. "The book becomes both an evocative work of rediscovery and a multilayered examination of how we tell contested stories" (White 1995, 31). Welch relays the infamous Battle of Little Bighorn within a literary frame that involves his discovery of the site of the Marias River massacre. This devastating incident for the Pikuni, Welch's ancestors, was a minor skirmish for the Cavalry, one of many forgotten massacres which are "rememoried," to borrow Toni Morrison's word from *Beloved* (1987, 215).

The horrific event that lived in Welch's memory and that is referenced in most of his works occurred in 1870; it was the massacre of the Blackfeet on the Marias River in Montana.

More than a century later, Welch was able to locate the physical site of the Marias River Massacre. In the early pages of *Killing Custer* he describes the journey. Accompanied by his wife Lois and his friend from the University of Montana, Bill Bevis, the three explorers set out to find the remnants of a destroyed Indian village, his great-grandmother's village. They were armed with a single faded photograph. All they could do was ask question after question until one farmer, who finally recognized a fencepost in the picture, pointed them in the direction of the place where Welch's Pikuni ancestors were slaughtered. Thus Welch couches the Battle of Little Bighorn within his own tribal experience, using research techniques much like the one just outlined: be personable; ask questions; hope for answers; don't take advantage of the informants. In Welch's imagination the Little Bighorn and the Marias rivers converge. The historic past has become the literary present. The end has become the beginning. The Marias River massacre, reenacted in Welch's memory and resurrected in *Killing Custer, Winter in the Blood,* and *Fools Crow,* has taken its rightful place.

Using the pattern of departure/return more fully defined in the next chapter, Welch circles back to the Marias River massacre (January 23, 1870) at the beginning of *Killing Custer* in order to locate himself, an Indian, within the endless domain of Indian time. At several key moments in the text Welch evokes two principal disasters: the Marias River massacre, which opens the book and the massacre at Wounded Knee, which closes it. Somewhat early in the book, for example, he describes what happened at Wounded Knee when, on December 29, 1890, the remnants of the Seventh Cavalry killed 300 Sioux men, women, and children. "They then threw the frozen corpses into a mass grave. With the last shovelful of dirt, Indian resistance to the white man in America effectively came to an end" (80). Wounded Knee represents the final incarceration of Indians in America. The last sentence of Welch's formal text repeats the earlier statement on page 80, ending with an ending: "Custer's old outfit had put an end to one of the greatest resistance movements in history" (271).

At the end of Chapter 8, Welch adds a note of bitter humor to the autobiographical tone with his account of meeting Russell Means. Means, the radical leader of the American Indian Movement, had challenged the glorified image of Custer in his own way in 1988 when he had erected a plaque on Last Stand Hill honoring those Indians who had defeated the Seventh Cavalry in the battle of Little Bighorn (Gildart 2001, 62). One night Means, whose long braids ostentatiously signified his Indianness, walked into the Elks Club where Welch, Stekler, and the video crew were having supper. Means showed hostility toward the project, asking Stekler pointed questions, wondering if the video would be just another film in which whites exploited Indians. Eventually Means loosened up. "He was Russell Means and he could not forget that, but he gave his image a rest for this one night," Welch remarks (226).

A week later Barbara Booher, the park superintendent who had brought Means to dinner, asked Welch if he would be interested in writing Means's biography. "She gave me his number, but I never called it," was his curt response (226). Welch's reason for declining the offer is vague, but two things seem apparent. First, his own career as a novelist was too important at that stage for him to become someone else's biographer. Second, whatever hostility Means showed toward the mild-mannered James Welch was reciprocated. In Welch's view the Battle of Little Bighorn is still causing divisions, even among Indians, "over a century later" (*Killing Custer* 1994, 226).

Many other authors have written about Little Bighorn, either to excuse Custer's errors or, like Welch, to restore the Indian to the center of the battlefield. One such book is *Little Bighorn Remembered,* published in 1999, five years after *Killing Custer.* This elegant production, 239 pages of text with page after page of full-color illustrations, battle drawings, maps, and pictograph engravings, was compiled by Herman J. Viola, Curator Emeritus of the Smithsonian. The flyleaf claims that *Little Bighorn Remembered* contains "an unprecedented oral history of the battle from the Native American point of view and the most comprehensive eyewitness description of Little Bighorn we have ever had." The Foreword, written by former park superintendent Gerard Baker claims: "Now at last *we* [emphasis his] are getting the opportunity to explain what happened" (xi).

I eagerly searched the index and the sparse bibliography for a reference to Welch's *Killing Custer*. No "James Welch" is listed. In *Additional Reading* (226–27) there is no reference either to *Killing Custer* or to *Last Stand at Little Bighorn*, the film Welch scripted with Paul Stekler. One cannot help but wonder why a scholar of Viola's stature, the adopted brother of Joseph Medicine Crow and the author of at least four books on the history of Indians in America, would deny the existence of a similar and earlier study by an Indian. Although certainly not as lavish as Viola's book, *Killing Custer* is dedicated to a similar project—to tell the story of "Custer's Last Stand" from an Indian perspective. As in the conflict between Welch and Means, perhaps someone had called Viola's attention to Welch's book but Viola had never responded. Even when the political direction is the same, the Custer question is capable of creating division, tension, and denial over a century later.

# 2

# Genres and Literary Heritage

James Welch, a student of the Fine Arts at the University of Montana, was aware of the fictional devices of Euro-American poets and novelists. At the same time he embraced the traditional Blackfeet beliefs found in narratives derived from oral tradition. As readers approach the individual chapters devoted to each of the novels they will become aware of Welch's expertise in mainstream narrative tradition: his persuasive use of plot, character, and structure; his photographer's sense of setting; his opulence of imagery. But they will also see that Welch descends from a Blackfeet oral tradition that relies on repeated motifs to convey a relatedness within the Indian community, a community of writers, Welch among them, whose values "still stand out in sharp contrast to the individualism, acquisitive materialism, and private capitalism of European America" (Olson and Wilson 1986, 313). As he learned from Richard Hugo, poets could wear blue jeans and buckskins. They could also resist the values of the dominant culture.

## RESERVATION HISTORY

Since Welch was born on the Blackfeet reservation in Browning, and since his most important novel, *Fools Crow*, is set at the junction between Indians being free and Indians being forced to live on reservations, it seems appropriate to give a brief account of how the reservation system developed historically in America and how it affected the Blackfeet. This account is based on a reliable but conservative source, *The Reservations* (Woodhead 1995).

Initial restrictions were greatest among Eastern tribes; the Penobscots of Maine, for example, were confined to several islands on the Penobscot River. Following the purchase of the Louisiana Territory from France in 1803, President Thomas Jefferson advocated a "policy of removal," arguing that the "removal" of Indians from the cramped Eastern states to the West would "provide protection from whites" and allow time for "assimilation" (Woodhead 1995, 30). This policy was enforced between 1789 and 1868, with Eastern tribes relocated mainly in Kansas, Oklahoma, and Arkansas. Intertribal wars broke out because some tribes, like the Osage, had already been living on the land for generations.

In 1825 James Monroe proposed moving all remaining Eastern Indians to Indian Country (Oklahoma and parts of Kansas and Nebraska). Three years later Andrew Jackson became president; the policy became law with the passage of the Indian Removal Act of 1830, which forced Southern tribes like the Choctaw, the Seminoles, and the Cherokees to surrender their lands and their lives.

The Great Plains Indians, including the Blackfeet, were the most resistant to these changes. Yet by the 1880s "some 360,000 Indians were contained on 441 federal reservations in 21 states and territories" (Woodhead 1995, 45). In 1883, after the buffalo had disappeared from the Plains, the government started to issue food and other supplies to the Blackfeet. Government intervention, as we learn from *Winter in the Blood* and other sources, was woefully inadequate. Many of the Blackfeet people starved to death during the winter of 1883–84; many others died of smallpox.

In an effort to stabilize so vast a territory after so dramatic an upheaval, the government passed the Dawes Act (the General Allotment Act) in 1887, ruling that the reservations would be partitioned and 16 acres reserved for each Indian family. Any unclaimed land was bought by the government; the government then sold the "excess" land to white settlers. Most Indian leaders opposed the Dawes Act, which dismantled the reservations and "tried to force Indians to assimilate with whites" (Beinart 1999, 35). Gradually the sense of identity as a nation was lost. The traditions and the language were forgotten. In a taped interview Welch said, "It's hard and almost impossible now to grasp that traditional past, except for some of the Indian peoples like the Navajo, some of the Pueblos, and some of the Sioux people" (*American Audio Prose Library* 1985).

## BLACKFEET TRADITIONAL NARRATIVES

One of the legends handed down orally for centuries is the Blackfeet account of creation. Like the writers of the book of Genesis in the Old Testament, many Blackfeet oral historians envision God as an Old Man. The God–Creator has been immortalized in Italian art through Michelangelo's famous bearded patriarch stretching his finger to ignite life into Adam. In the Blackfeet oral tradition, although the Great Spirit is responsible for the creation of man and woman, Old Man is simply there: "No one made Old Man; he always existed" (Wissler and Duvall [1908] 1995, 23).

In a number of tales Old Man exhibits the characteristics of the trickster. The trickster is an ambiguous figure who appears in various folk cultures. Usually he takes the form of an animal—a coyote, a raven, a bear. Anthropologist Zora Neale Hurston wrote about the African American trickster, which derived from west Africa: "The rabbit, the bear, the lion, the buzzard, the fox are culture heroes from the animal world" (Hurston 1934, 36). According to K. L. Nichols, the Native American Indian trickster is a complex and ambivalent figure who "alternately scandalizes, disgusts, amuses, disrupts, chastises, and humiliates (or is humiliated by) the animal-like proto-people of pre-history, yet he is also a creative force transforming their world, sometimes in bizarre and outrageous ways, with his instinctive energies and cunning" (Nichols 1).

Old Man (Na'pi) is a creative force capable of transformation or metamorphosis. In one strange and admittedly confusing story the people pray to Old Man because they are hungry and there is no game to be found. Na'pi and a young man discover a lone Indian who has hidden the buffalo and the other animals. Old Man changes himself into a dog and the young man changes himself into a root-digger or painted stick. Later the dog and the stick find a herd of buffalo in a cave and drive many of them into the prairie. Infuriated, the buffalo-hoarder tries to kill them but they ride safely from the cave under an animal's dense hair, an escape that will remind Western readers of Odysseus's tricking the Cyclops by riding under the belly of a sheep. Next Old Man changes himself into a beaver, plays dead, and captures a raven, who is the buffalo-hoarder in disguise. As the raven is about to die from being hung over a smoke-hole, Old Man reverts to his former shape and says: "I cannot die. Look at me! Of all peoples and tribes I am the chief. I cannot die. I made the mountains." He tells the raven to go home and hunt for his family like the rest of the tribe or face extinction (Grinnell [1892] 1962, 145–48).

This story involves a fourfold metamorphosis in the figures of the dog, the raven, the beaver, and the stick, with the stick inexplicably disappearing at some point in the narrative. For our purposes the tale is useful on several levels. First, it reflects the disjointed structure of Welch's earliest novel, *Winter in the Blood*. Second, it reveals the ambiguous or two-sided nature of Old Man, a literary prototype who, like Mik-api of *Fools Crow*, can be both healing and vindictive. Third, in its multilayered reference to animals, "The Dog and the Stick" is one of several Blackfeet narratives that serves as a model for a central argument of this book: namely, that in his novels animals inform and enhance such literary components as theme, structure, plot, and characterization.

For Welch and other Indian novelists, Na'pi's complex nature would offer an enticement for theme and characterization. George Bird Grinnell describes him as "a mixture of wisdom and foolishness; he is malicious, selfish, childish, and weak" ([1913] 1926, 156). When he gets in trouble he often calls on animals to help him. Na'pi's need for assistance from animal-helpers is echoed by many of Welch's characters, while the teaching attribute of Old Man is evident in the grandfather or shaman characters of *Winter in the Blood* and *Fools Crow*. Welch recalls how the elders of his tribe, especially his grandmother, used to teach him magical tales of ducks, muskrats, and other animals (*Native American Novelists Series* 1999).

There are numerous references in Blackfeet mythology to animals as sacred creatures possessing powers greater than man's. In one version of the creation story, the birds and the animals are there at the beginning, before the appearance of men and women. To help people survive Old Man makes the grass to grow and the roots to flourish. He teaches hunting and healing and carries a medicine bag (Wissler and Duvall [1908] 1995, 23). In a more ominous version of the myth, Old Man, after teaching the Blackfeet about survival, warns them to keep strangers out of their territory, an injunction that they ignore. By letting enemies enter their land, the Blackfeet have disobeyed Old Man's warning (Grinnell [1892] 1962, 137–45; see also "The Blackfoot Genesis" in Feldmann 1965, 73–79). The ominous warning against trusting one's enemy is reiterated in the prophetic conclusion of *Fools Crow*.

## ANIMALS

In *Blackfoot Lodge Tales*, George Bird Grinnell provides an extensive list of animals respected by the Plains Indians, including the buffalo, geese, the bear, the raven, and the wolf. The wandering wolf, Grinnell explains, was the friend of the nomadic tribes, while the raven was esteemed for his ability to locate an enemy or indicate the presence of game ([1892] 1962, 260–62). Grinnell recounts how Old Man instructed the earliest people to hunt buffalo and small game, telling them that they will get power from animals who appear to them in dreams: "Whatever these animals tell you to do, you must obey them, as they appear to you in your sleep. Be guided by them. . . . It may be by the eagles, perhaps by the buffalo, or by the bears. Whatever animal answers your prayer, you must listen to him" (Grinnell [1892] 1962, 141).

In a number of myths domesticated animals possess magical powers. Old Man, disguised as a dog, is able to outwit the buffalo-hoarder in "The Dog and the Stick." In "The Lost Children" an old woman's pet dog is able to follow her instructions and bite through the ropes of two young victims in bondage, leading them to food and warning them not to enter their parents' camp (Grinnell [1892] 1962, 50–60). Dogs are not always heroic, though. In the morbid story, "Why Dogs Do Not Talk," a dog spies a medicine woman meeting her lover at night and tells the betrayed husband. In anger the woman makes the dog eat human excrement. After this, while dogs could "understand some words," they could not talk (Wissler and Duvall [1908] 1995, 133).

Before the introduction of the horse, dogs were used to haul bundles and even infants on a large, attached cart called the travois (Grinnell [1892] 1962, 187). Dogs guarded the lodges and gave warning when an enemy approached. They were, then and now, a source of companionship, as witnessed in "The Lost Children" and other stories. The theme of the dog as companion is most evident in the figure of Swipsey in Welch's *The Death of Jim Loney*.

The horse was introduced to the American continent by the Spaniards in the 1540s (Taylor 1997, 18). Eventually horses came to the Plains Indians, to the Crow and then to the Blackfeet, replacing the dog as the primary work animal. In *Killing Custer* Welch emphasizes the enormous change that the horse made to the Blackfeet way of life. So much more powerful than the dog, the horse was useful to the Plains Indians for hunting and hauling. It increased the mobility of the tribes, making the hunting of buffalo and moving from summer to winter camp less arduous. The more horses one had, the more wives; the more wives the more tanned buffalo skins for trading (*Killing Custer* 1994, 138–40). Above all, the horse represented a new idea for the Indian–"that it was desirable to accumulate property" (Grinnell [1982] 1962, 243).

From a mythological perspective, the horse is related to the vision quest, since he is often the creature who carries the dream-seeker to the sacred ground. In one Arapaho myth a Medicine man, Dreamwalker, journeys to the land of the wild stallions. He talks to four horses of four colors—Black, Yellow, Red, and White—receiving messages and gifts so that he can heal his people (Sams and Carson 1988, 177–78). The Sioux shaman Black Elk records a complex vision of horses when, at the age of nine, he is transported on a whirl of clouds to see twelve black horses with necklaces of bison's hoofs; twelve white horses circled by geese; twelve sorrels; and twelve buckskins. "And yonder suddenly the sky was terrible with a storm of plunging horses of all colors that shook the world with thunder, neighing back" (Neihardt [1932] 1998, 24). As the horses plunge and the clouds become a rainbow, Black Elk meets the six grandfathers, each of them an aspect of Old Man. In a series of related visions, Black Elk sees the great hoop of the earth rise and break. At the end of his ascent over the mountains the sun sings to him and an eagle guides him home. Where he had once seen a flaming rainbow he now sees the mountains; where he had once heard the Voice of the Great Spirit he now sees his parents tending to him as he recovers from his trance (Neihardt [1932] 1998, 20–47). The horse is prominent in *Winter in the Blood*.

Here, I explore the relevance of animals as they relate to Welch's poetry and to each of his novels, from the curious menagerie of cows and horses, of ducks and talking deer in *Winter in the Blood* to the disenfranchised title character of *The Heartsong of Charging Elk*, the elk being an animal assimilated with great frequency into Indian naming practices. Because the Indian fascination with the power of visionary animals is at the core of Welch's first three works of fiction, this study highlights his references to animals in the novels and draws attention to their importance elsewhere—in his poetry, his fiction, and his nonfiction, even in two of his titles, *Fools Crow* and *The Heartsong of Charging Elk*.

## THE VISION QUEST

Among the Lakota Sioux and other Indian tribes of the Northern Plains there was a sacred ritual known as the vision quest. This ritual was initiated by a young man who, after seeking counsel from a holy man, entered the sweat lodge to be purified. He then went to a remote place where he could achieve a spiritual state without worldly distraction. Here he prayed and fasted, going to the center pole of his lodge and moving in each of the four directions, sometimes facing the Sun, in a ceremony that lasted from two to four days. At times he received advice from an animal, who became his special helper. He then gathered physical proof of the vision into his medicine bag for future protection. When returning from the vision quest the "seeker" carried parts of the guardian spirit in his bundle or pouch during later rituals at the sweat lodge (Versluis 1999, 64–66; see also "Religion" in thewildwest.org). A number of Blackfeet legends are structured on the vision quest; one that appears frequently is the story of Poia or Scarface (see the version recorded by Walter McClintock [1999, 491–505]). The vision quest is crucial to an understanding of *Fools Crow.*

The quest pattern, which is central to such European masterpieces as *The Odyssey* and *The Aeneid,* is a fundamental aspect of Native American literature, from the Blackfeet Old Man tales to N. Scott Momaday's prize-winning novel *The House Made of Dawn.* The quest usually involves both a physical journey and a search for survival in an alien world. Because the quest motif exists both in the European and the Indian traditions, the critic must be aware of Welch's double heritage: "he is widely read in Western European literature and is an Indian who has lived on a reservation" (Ruoff 1978, Discussion Session, 165).

In Welch's novels the quest generally focuses on the male hero's search for the father/grandfather or, on a larger scale, for tribal identity. As we shall see, the quest demands that the protagonist leave his homeland until, through a series of events or challenges, he is worthy to return to his people. Welch employs the idea of the departure/quest/return most ironically in *The Heartsong of Charging Elk,* where the hero, a Lakota Sioux stranded in France, refuses the chance to return to America.

The seemingly disjointed structure of Welch's first three novels can be viewed as a reflection of his Blackfeet literary heritage, gleaned from the quest-narratives told to him by his elders and collected more formally by Grinnell, Duvall, and other ethnographers. In many of the old stories the protagonist experiences confusing physical and emotional changes. In the story of Mik-api, for example, the hero goes scalp-collecting in a quest to avenge two widows whose husbands had been killed by the Snake tribe. While asleep in a cave, Mik-api feels a hand touching him and knows it is a Snake warrior. He kills the Snake, then has a dream in which he sees an eagle dropping a snake to the ground. Mik-api is struck by an arrow and falls into the river, wounded, until he is rescued by a grizzly, who packs him in mud. The trickster/hero rides home on the bear's back and is met with shouting and dancing. He then marries two young sisters and lives to be the "greatest" of all chiefs. "He did many other great and daring things" (Grinnell, [1892] 1962, 61–69).

The story of Mik-api is patterned on the quest, with the hero in search of defending the bereft widows of his tribe. As a hero he participates in the larger quest for acceptance within the Blackfeet community. The narrative scatters from place to place, with many omissions and no finite resolution. Names and titles are obscure. The bear-helper who saves the hero appears out of nowhere. To a non-Indian reader the narrative might appear to be incoherent, much like the vision dream of Black Elk. Or, as Susan Feldmann comments in her Introduction to *The Storytelling Stone:* "Perhaps most trickster tales are too rambling and pointless to suit our Western taste" (Feldmann 1965, 19).

Western readers seem to demand a beginning, a middle, and a resolution, whereas Indian tales, chants, and ceremonies usually reject this pattern. They are cyclical in nature, moving the participant not from the beginning to the end but from the beginning back to the beginning. Arthur Versluis describes the symbol of the cross within the tree, the tree representing the four seasons of "traditional time cycles" and the circle the "cyclical nature" of traditional systems of the universe (1999, 103–04). Paula Gunn Allen calls this cyclical pattern "the sacred hoop," a phrase immortalized by Black Elk in his autobiography: "In the old days when we were a strong and happy people, all our power came to us from the sacred hoop of the nation, and so long as the hoop was unbroken, the people flourished. . . . Everything the power of the world does is done in a circle" (Neihardt [1932] 1998, 194). Black Elk lists the sun, the moon, the seasons, the birds, the wind, the stars as parts of the sacred hoop. Man, too, is contained within this holy circularity. "The life of man is a circle from childhood to childhood, and so is everything where power moves" (Neihardt [1932] 1998, 195).

If the life of man is symbolized by the circle, then the reader should expect to find elements of that sacred hoop in the plot development of Indian writers. The pattern of return demands that the hero, who for one reason or another has left the community or the reservation, must eventually come home in order to reestablish the circle so vital to Indian spirituality. In Welch's fiction the central characters, all of whom are males, leave their communities, either to attend law school or to rescue a wolverine or to join up with Buffalo Bill. With the exception of Charging Elk, their quests lead them back to their ancestral traditions.

The structural element of the quest is inextricably bonded to the plot element of the return. William Bevis argues that the "homing" pattern in Indian literature involves a different plot design than what one finds in European and American fiction. Euro/American characters reach out toward an individualized future that rejects the past, whereas contemporary

Indian characters come home to reestablish their identity with the people (Bevis 1993, 19). The film *Medicine River* (1994) offers an excellent contemporary application of the pattern of return. *Medicine River* involves a successful photographer, Will, played by Graham Greene, and his return to a small town near Calgary after his mother's death. *Medicine River* thus succeeds in its depiction of a "lost boy returning home" (Kilpatrick 1999, 206).

The "homing" pattern is obviously present in non-Indian literature. The Prodigal Son of the New Testament, who has left home for the city, returns repentantly to his family; Odysseus, blown off course after the Trojan War, returns to his wife and son to reclaim his lost kingship. In some rare instances the return is performed by a woman, as in Charlotte Bronte's *Jane Eyre* (1847). Jane, discovering that her intended bridegroom is already married, leaves Rochester's estate to reestablish her respectability. When she eventually returns, Jane learns that Rochester's wife is dead and Rochester blind. In a reversal of the typical male/female pattern, it is the woman who returns to regenerate her dependent lover. While Welch's plots are based on an ambivalent version of the lost son's—and not the daughter's—homecoming, they strongly invoke this pattern of return.

## *MITAKUYE OYASIN*—"ALL ARE RELATED"

In his novels Welch uses animals to signify interconnection or relatedness. Among the Lakota Sioux of South Dakota there is a revered phrase, *"mitakuye oyasin,"* which translates as "all are related." The Sioux and other Indians of the Northern Plains continue to honor the same integral connections among people, animals, and the natural world that abounded in the ancient myths and tales. *Mitakuye oyasin* "includes every human being on this earth, every animal down to the tiniest insect, and every living plant" (Erdoes and Ortiz 1999, xix). In 1999 the concept was cited in an objection to the proposed construction of a hog farm on the Rosebud Reservation in South Dakota. Pigs raised on large farms, one dissenter argued, were subject to physical disorders, misshapen legs, and suffocation. This inhumane treatment of hogs was "in direct contrast to the Lakota belief of 'mitakuye oyasin' or 'all my relations,'—the belief that all life, including the animal world, is related" (Kent, a2). Leonard Peltier, the Sioux activist tried and found guilty for his alleged participation in the 1975 killings of two FBI agents, invokes the holy phrase in the epilogue and in the conclusion of *Prison Writings:* "Perhaps we'll meet one day, you

24 James Welch

and I, on the Great Red Road. I pray that we do. *Mitakuye Oyasin!*" (Peltier 2000, 212).

Joseph Epes Brown, who lived on the Pine Ridge reservation in South Dakota in the 1940s, wrote a definitive study of *mitakuye oyasin* and its relevance to the Sioux concept of "underlying connections" or "relationship" (Brown 1997, 97–98). To my knowledge there is no comparable study of Blackfeet ideology, although Allen C. Ross (1989) and other major scholars of Lakota Sioux philosophy have interpreted this term to apply not only to the Sioux but to all Native Americans, despite any further differences in language, ritual, or mythology.

Like the Sioux, the Blackfeet and Gros Ventre tribes of Montana have shared a respect for the actual and symbolic power of animals and for their relatedness with humans. Curly Bear Wagner, a Blackfeet tribal historian, told a reporter for the *Glacier Guide:* "Our people believe that everything is living; the mountains, trees, grass, dirt, and water are all related, and we (people) are part of that relationship" (Habets 2002, 4). Joseph Campbell says much the same thing in the *Power of Myth:* "The Indians addressed all of life as a 'thou'—the trees, the stones, everything" (Campbell 1991, 99.)

When I asked Welch if there was a similar phrase among the Blackfeet for *mitakuye oyasin*, he explained that while he could not recall an equivalent term, the concept was the same: "Being part of the tribe is living in harmony and identifying with the natural world around you. Everything, from the rocks to the mountains, has a soul, has a quality to them" ("Montana Interview").

## POETRY

In 1971 Welch's poetry, which focused on contemporary Indian life in Montana, was collected into a short volume titled *Riding the Earthboy 40.* The word *earthboy* means farmer or tender of the earth, much as "cowboy" means a person who tends cattle. The Earthboys were also a family who leased 40 acres next to his parents' ranch (Lee 1994, 194). "Riding" evokes the obvious image of a man on horseback but also suggests the "ghost rider" or shaman/poet. The volume, which contains 53 poems, is divided into four sections. The second section, "The Renegade Wants Words," contains the greatest number of poems (16), as well as the title poem for the volume and Welch's best-known poem, "The Man from Washington." His poetry, like his novels, is informed by both a Euro-American literary tradition and a Blackfeet oral heritage.

Welch's mentor, Richard Hugo, assigned Welch to read modern writers like Theodore Roethke (1908–1963), William Butler Yeats (1865–1939), Wallace Stevens (1879–1955), and other writers whose poems had become the literary standard in graduate programs across America. If Welch was to learn the craft, he had to read the masters. Welch's poetry is complicated by a highly sophisticated language and by poetic forms and images adopted by mainstream poets of the early to mid-twentieth century. Although very little of it could be called autobiographical, it bears Welch's handprint because of its Native American orientation.

The lovely poem "Arizona Highways" has affinities with Wallace Stevens, with William Wordsworth, with Richard Hugo, and with Welch's first novel, *Winter in the Blood.* Apparently recalling the opening lines of Wallace Stevens's "The Idea of Order at Key West," it is told from the perspective of a persona or fictionalized first-person narrator—a traveler, a migrant farmer, or perhaps an itinerant minister—presumably not Welch himself. The narrator is intrigued by a 17-year old woman wearing a turquoise bracelet. She is separated from the persona by a distance that is both cultural and emotional. The resolution is blunt, straightforward: "I'll move on" (19). After a series of sexual fantasies, he leaves the girl and moves on to a home as remote as "the cloud I came in on" (19). If one mentally substitutes the word "horse" for the Romantic word "cloud," the last line is toying with a classical image from the Westerns: the horse he rode in on.

Richard Hugo, director of the Writing Program at University of Montana, was an exemplary poet and educator. He had discovered in his prize student a rare kind of American poet—an American Indian who had been born on a reservation far from the cultural trappings of the standard curriculum, a blank page on which to inscribe the names of Yeats and Roethke. Hugo's poem "The Lady in Kicking Horse Reservoir," published in 1973, two years after Welch's *Riding the Earthboy 40,* seems to have benefited from his own exposure to Indian legend and history; it refers to the Flathead Indian Reservation and to the cries of drowned Indians (Ferguson, Salter, and Stallworthy 1996, 1570–71).

Hugo encouraged Welch to describe what he already knew, the towns and reservations of Montana, using the language and perceptions of contemporary Indians. "Hugo, in his infinite wisdom and generosity, said, 'Go ahead, write about the reservation, the landscape, the people'" (Introduction, *Third Catalog of Native American Literature* 1997, 2). Following Hugo's advice and his own instincts, Welch began to focus on the people and objects in his immediate environment: bar scenes in Harlem and

Dixon, naming, drunks, porcupines, clouds, bones, horses, coyotes, tumbleweed, Indian women.

As in all of his writing, animals play a prominent role in his poetry. In the poem "Snow Country Weavers" a bird returns from the south to tell the poet that wolves are dying from the cold and that spiders are weaving webs "filled with words" (*Riding the Earthboy 40*, 47). Readers familiar with the talking raven of *Fools Crow* will not be surprised at the way spiders and talking birds contribute meaning to this otherwise puzzling poem. References to animals appear on nearly every page of the collected poetry, ranging from common inhabitants of the environment, such as bull snakes, fish, dogs, and wolves, to mythical reminders of the past, as in the poem "Blackfeet, Blood, and Piegan Hunters," where white buffalo have left their tracks for future storytellers (36).

Profound associations between Indians and animals are of course not exclusive to Welch's works but are woven throughout contemporary Indian poetry. There are many animal references in *Harper's Anthology of 20th Century Native American Poetry* (Niatum 1988), among them Ray A. Young Bear's "The First Dimension of Skunk" (257–61); Joy Harjo's "She Had Some Horses" (284–85); Harjo's "Eagle Poem," with its dizzying, circular motion (297); N. Scott Momaday's "The Bear" (63); and James Welch's "Magic Fox" (138).

Another noticeable feature of Welch's poetry, one that predicts his shift to novelistic form, is that so many of the poems tell stories or address the craft of storytelling. "In My Lifetime" is about a man whose "bleeding feet" record a history of sin and creation, of living in the forest, of "winter in the blood" (27), the phrase that was to become the title of Welch's first novel and that marked his definitive break from poetry into narrative fiction. Kenneth Lincoln connects the storyteller of "In My Lifetime" to Na'pi or Old Man, who gave breath to the first people much as Welch has given breath to the rhythms of oral poetry (Lincoln 1979, 34). In "Blackfeet, Blood and Piegan Hunters" the poetic voice ironically identifies with the storytelling of his ancestors. For the modern poet the tribal definitions have vanished and the poets now "dance for pennies" (36). The self-deprecating tone recalls another poem, "D-Y Bar," in which Bear Child, a storyteller, acts out or plays bear on all four paws in order to get drinks from his white audience (38).

The voice in most of the poems is the "I," the Indian condemned to a life of struggle and poverty but smart enough and angry enough to be a renegade/poet. A few of the poems are told from the point of view of an "I" speaking to a "You," as in the anti-assimilation poem "Plea to Those

Who Matter," where the Indian poet promises to please his captor by burning his drum, cutting his hair, and smashing his crooked nose. Like the nose, the narrative voice in Welch's "plea" is sharp and defiant. Its sharpness is uncharacteristic of most of Welch's more elegant poetry.

When we talked with Welch in Montana, Ken Baldwin asked him about a strange poem titled "The World's Only Corn Palace" (17), a reference to an architectural oddity located in Mitchell, South Dakota. Each year a community of local residents changes the facade of the building, creating a new design made entirely of corn. Neither of us could figure out what the poem, with its violent images of "knives and sticks" and initials "carved" on the victim's heart, really had to do with the Corn Palace. Jim gave an ironic trickster response: "Actually, it just has to do with the 'corny' sentiments in the poem. It really doesn't have anything to do with the Corn Palace because it's a corny poem about poets" ("Montana Interview").

It is of course dangerous to read too much into any poem, corn or no corn, and Welch's curious place names and locales can often throw readers off. Brian Swann mistakenly connects the poem "Harlem, Montana: Off the Reservation" with Harlem, New York, claiming that Welch is linking "one place of dissatisfaction in Montana with another in New York, indict[ing] a whole country" (Swann, in Niatum 1988, xxiii). *Harlem*, however, is a Dutch word, and many of the early settlers of New York and Montana were of Dutch descent. The poem mentions Hutterites, a group like the Mennonites. These religious communal sects wear black but aren't Black. If the meanings of Welch's poems are not always intelligible, the problem stems not only from our own cultural unfamiliarity with small Montana towns but also from Welch's advocacy of the "nonmeaning" of much twentieth-century poetry, exemplified in Archibald MacLeish's famous 1926 statement: "A poem should not mean/But be" (Ferguson, Salter, and Stallworthy, 1271).

Looking at Welch's indigenous roots, critics often enter unsettled terrain. From general sources we know that the poetry of the ancient tribes, with its rhythms of drum beats and claps of thunder, was an aspect of ritual in which being, dance, and physical participation dominated meaning. In *The Sky Clears*, Grove A. Day characterizes Native American poetry as being primarily religious or ritualistic, involving repetition and chanting. Day also cites several war chants composed by Plains warriors that call on birds, wolves, and other natural allies for strength in battle. Welch occasionally approximates the rhythms of traditional Indian poetry through the use of chant and repetition, as in the poems "Picnic Weather" (12) and

"The Versatile Historian" (54). But Kenneth Lincoln exaggerates Welch's style when he describes him as speaking with the "shaman's tongue, mysterious and ritualistic, chanting in strange, concentrated phrases, in paradox and parable" (Lincoln 1979, 33). Lincoln's tribute to Welch's Native poetics tends to miss out on the individualized points of view and the barroom language, the earthboy tones of the cloud Welch rode in on. Lincoln is reluctant to credit Welch's tight style to his connections with Roethke, Yeats, and other modernists who were Welch's acknowledged mentors. At its best Welch's poetry captures an Indian vision of the landscape—its jagged features; its flow, its mountains and rivers, its circularity, its relatedness—in a pattern of intricate design and formal elegance that owes much to Richard Hugo.

No discussion of Welch's poetry should end without looking at "The Man from Washington." As far as his poetry goes, "The Man From Washington" is, Welch admitted, "by far the most accessible" ("Montana Interview"). The first line of this forceful poem deals directly with the ending of the Blackfeet nation and with the people's confinement on the reservation, which "came easy for most of us" (*Riding the Earthboy 40*, 35). Welch uses the word *easy* for its ultimately ironic effect; there was nothing "easy" about the end of freedom and the end of a self-determined life. The man in the title, a bureaucrat representing the federal government, is a dwarflike emissary with "rainwater eyes" who made treaties that were broken and promises that were never kept. The poem is written in past tense to convey a flat and finished history. The singular man of the title dominates the poem and its people, who are the collective "we" or "us"— the victimized. This short and bitter poem, so concise in its phrasing, is not typical of Welch's more modulated style. Its historical emphasis predicts the narrative strategy of both *Killing Custer* and *Fools Crow*.

## FILM

Most Americans have learned about Indians through movies. The stereotyping of Native Americans in the film industry is the subject of two major academic books, *Celluloid Indians* (Kilpatrick 1999) and *Hollywood's Indian* (Rollins and O'Connor 1998). Kilpatrick takes film from the John Ford stage to the waters of *Medicine River* in an elaborate guide that helps viewers evaluate the way Indians are portrayed in a movie. Both books examine conventional views of Indians in film and question our assumptions of what was called "the Noble Savage" or just "the Savage." Ken Nolley generalizes: "Like other westerns, too, all of Ford's plots, with the exception of *Cheyenne Autumn*, construct Indians as a savage presence set in opposition to the advance of American civilization, particularly as that civilization is embodied in white families" (Rollins and O'Connor 1998, 80).

Many of the countless films about George Armstrong Custer belong to the "Indian as Savage" genre. In *They Died with Their Boots On* (1941) Errol Flynn's Custer is played out against Anthony Quinn's Crazy Horse. "As Crazy Horse rides down upon and kills Custer, the audience sees a savage killing machine mowing down a righteous and courageous 'real American'" (Kilpatrick 1999, 52). Even when Custer is portrayed as an irresponsible officer, the scales still tend to tilt toward the rights of settlers and the vigilance of the Seventh Cavalry, with historical facts based on newspaper accounts, journals, and other written documents.

Welch's most significant contribution to film is his debunking of the Custer myth in *Last Stand at Little Bighorn*. In this PBS script, coauthored with Paul Stekler and produced by WGBH/Boston, Welch attacks the image of the savage scalp-hunter and retells the events of June 26, 1876, through an accumulation of data based primarily on Indian accounts told orally by ancestors of the Sioux, Cheyenne, and other tribes.

Welch described his initial involvement to me. "A filmmaker [Paul Stekler] called me from Boston and said he's gotten my name. Would I be interested in helping him to write a script for a movie which would have as its central point the battle of Little Bighorn?" Welch countered that he had only "a layman's knowledge of that battle. I've been to the battlefield a couple of times but I don't know much about it." But after doing research, he agreed to tackle the script. "We batted out several scripts, going back and forth from Boston to Missoula. The film was shown on the American Experience, I think in 1992."

*Last Stand at Little Bighorn* is narrated by N. Scott Momaday. It begins with an opening statement testifying to the hundreds of Sioux and Cheyenne warriors who survived the Battle of Little Bighorn, fought on the plains of southern Montana. Approximately 260 of the invaders died, some of them trained soldiers, most of them farm boys. The most inglorious of the dead was George Armstrong Custer.

A film clip of Errol Flynn playing Custer is followed by a series of pictographs—abstract Indian visual representations of history. Viewers learn that Custer, last in his class at West Point, had been responsible for the massacre of more than 100 Indians at the Washita River in the Indian Territory of Oklahoma in 1868 when he and the Seventh Cavalry invaded a friendly village of Southern Cheyenne and slaughtered the women and

children, the horses and dogs. They burned 51 lodges and shot Chief Black
Kettle and his wife, Medicine Woman Later, as they attempted to escape
(Welch, *Killing Custer* 1994, 61–64). In 1873, unsettled by the collapse in
the economy, the government decided that the Indian Wars would "do no
harm." Ten years later it sent the Seventh Calvary into the Black Hills to
guide an expedition of 25,000 miners who had come in search of gold.

At that point the video shifts to an almost exclusively Indian perspective
that highlights Sitting Bull's vision of soldiers falling upside down from
the sky. It features Crazy Horse, not Custer, as the true hero of the battle.
It also deals honestly with the internal rivalry between the Sioux and the
Crows, a Montana tribe that sided with Custer because they had been
pushed back by the Lakota Sioux. The battle is bloody, and one can almost
smell the stench of the naked bodies: "Oh, how white they looked, how
white." The script next follows Sitting Bull to Canada and Crazy Horse,
the great Sioux warrior, to the reservation stockade, where he was stabbed
to death.

There are a number of elements that one immediately associates with
Welch. First and most immediate are the power of the narrative and the
vivid characterization. The viewer also notices the persistent use of animal
imagery—the magpies in the sky, the piles of buffalo bones, Chief Spotted
Horse's vision of more and more whites entering the territory "like ants."
At the end of the film Welch and Stekler emphasize that the notorious
Battle of Little Bighorn was but one of many wars fought between the
Indians and settlers during the Indian Wars.

The research done for the video was eventually incorporated into the
1994 book, *Killing Custer*. Like his novels, so Welch's piece of historical
nonfiction tends to move in and out of time and space. In an important
interview William Bevis commends Welch for his use of "circular time"
and for constructing *Killing Custer* through a "cycling of repetitions"
("Wylie Tales" 1995, 11). Bevis captures the sense of sublime confusion
the reader feels as he or she reads forwards and backwards, with the
Indians gathering off and on, again and again. What Bevis modestly over-
looks is that he too is a participant in the "anti-narrative structure" ("Wylie
Tales" 1995, 11), since the initial project was spawned by his visit with Jim
and Lois Welch in the fall of 1985.

Welch's moving book is enriched by his readable style and his persuasive argumentation. The reviewer for *Booklist*, for example, found *Killing
Custer* to be "both interesting and well written" (Freeman 1994, 477). The
reviewer for *The New Statesman* commended it for being "evocatively and
compellingly written" (Carr 1995, 39). The verbal excellence is augmented

by the budding technology of photographs—of General Custer, of General Sherman, of Bloody Knife, one of Custer's scouts. One extraordinary photo shows some men being dwarfed by a pile of buffalo skulls (76). These visual images, complemented with the ledger drawings of Short Bull, Sitting Bull, and other Indian historians, appear in the video.

Welch converted many of the vivid film images into dramatic passages—the choking clouds of dust during the battle, the mutilation of Custer's brother Tom, the stripping and scalping of dead soldiers. Welch's power of description abounds. With remarkable directness he writes: "Crazy Horse knew he was a prisoner" (249). After being taken to Fort Robinson, the guards threw the Sioux warrior into the stockade, "a small building next to the adjunct's. When he entered he saw bars, a small high window. He smelled the stench of urine. He knew it was an iron house" (251). Attempting to escape from his "iron house," which in prisons would be called the "hole," Crazy Horse is stabbed by a guard "again and again, deep in the side, then in the back" (251). For Crazy Horse and most Native Americans, the reservation is in fact a prison, a place of detention, despair, and death. In both the video and the book these ideas emerge.

Although he expressed a great interest in films like *Smoke Signals* and *Powwow Highway,* and although he was pleased that some of his novels had been optioned for film, Welch confessed his reluctance to shift to this media: "I don't do film. I've been asked many times to help write scripts" ("Baltimore Interview").

## The Back Side of the Camera

During the past several decades, thanks to Welch and other scriptwriters, there has been a more honest portrayal of the historical Indian. *Thunderheart* (1992), written by John Fusco and directed by Michael Apted, is set on the Pine Ridge Reservation of South Dakota during government investigations following the death of two FBI agents in the 1970s. In this very real incident the villains are the FBI. The heroes are a tribal cop, played with typical brilliance by Graham Greene, and Val Kilmer, an FBI agent who in the course of his investigation discovers his Sioux heritage. *Thunderheart* thus avoids the problem found in Kevin Costner's *Dances with Wolves* (1990) and John Woo's *Windtalkers* (2002), in which the narrative explores the sensibilities of a white central character.

In Welch's opinion, the "main problem of *Dances with Wolves* is the homogeneity, the interchangeability of the Indian characters" (*Killing Custer* 1994, 99). Although a few of the actors are distinctive, most are merely in the background, with too much time "spent loving Kevin Costner's face" (*Killing Custer* 1994, 99). *Dances with Wolves* won the Oscar for Best Picture and Best Director in 1990. Despite its shortcomings, its vast popularity and frequent replay on television have helped to create a better, if imperfect, understanding of life on the Plains in the post–Civil War period.

A more unusual category includes films starring Native Americans or scripted by Native Americans. Many have a documentary style, as in Michael Apted's *Incident in Oglala* (1991), the story of the murder of the same two FBI agents who illegally entered the Pine Ridge Indian reservation in South Dakota in 1975 (the aftermath of which is covered in *Thunderheart* [1992]). "The incident stemmed from continuous unrest in the area following the battles between AIM [the American Indian Movement] and the corrupt Pine Ridge Tribal Council" (Pritzker 2000, 335). The film documents the story of Indian leader Leonard Peltier, who was found guilty and sentenced to life in prison. Another excellent but little known documentary, *Paha Sapa: The Struggle for the Black Hills* (1993), describes the willful destruction of sacred Sioux land during the Gold Rush and, a century later, in the tourism trade. It is narrated by Russell Means and other Sioux activists, lawyers, and educators. Welch's historically based script on the Battle of Little Bighorn belongs in this category of documentary films and videos.

In recent years Hollywood has relied on the talents of actor Adam Beach to depict the Indian much as in the 1950s and 1960s it had relied on John Wayne to depict the Cowboy. Beach played the lead role in *Squanto* (Disney 1993), a surprisingly sympathetic film about an Indian who is captured and brutally treated by the English. In a film that vigorously challenges racial stereotypes, Sidney Poitier and Adam Beach play a Black man and an Indian who die together at the hands of a vigilante team (*A Good Day to Die*, 1995). In Chris Eyre's made-for-television movie *Skinwalker* (2002), Adam Beach pairs with Wes Studi, the brilliant star of *Geronimo*, as Navajo tribal policemen searching for a trickster who has been murdering medicine men. They discover that the villain is really a modern doctor who fears that he will be unable to treat the sick as long as superstitions prevail. Beach is also the much applauded star of *Windtalkers*. This film, released in 2002, received mixed reviews. Many critics thought there was too much guilt-ridden Nicolas Cage and not nearly enough heroic Adam Beach in his role as a Navajo code-talker during the Second World War. But the reviewer for *Native Peoples* admired *Windtalkers* because it exposed so many filmgoers to the important contributions made by Native Americans in the Pacific (Iglesias 2002, 90–93). Beach is also doing a film about a modern Indian on a Harley Davidson, directed by John Rice and produced by Nicolas Cage (Noel 2002, 41–44).

There are many other films of merit. *Billy Jack* (1971) makes a serious attempt to convey Native American life and customs. Another tribal cop, Billy Jack defends his people against the greedy settlers who want horses, land, and control. In the movie he performs a Snake Ceremony, carries a medicine pouch, and revives the Ghost Dance, which was an "Indian religion that promised a return to a prewhite Indian paradise" (Pritzker 2000, 295). Unfortunately, much of the movie is contrived or poorly acted. A contemporary film that would have a vast appeal for younger audiences is *War Party* (1989). Set in Welch's Montana, it begins with the townspeople re-enacting an historic battle between the Cavalry and the Blackfeet. When one of the soldiers uses real bullets and kills an Indian teenager, two of his friends seek revenge. Like *A Good Day to Die,* the film ends with a vigilante group killing the two avengers, played by Billy Wirth and Kevin Dillon.

There is another kind of movie that gives one hope of a new direction in film. This genre would identify films completely controlled by Native peoples in terms of acting, script, technical production, and directing. Although the film *House Made of Dawn* (1996) was based on the novel by N. Scott Momaday and starred Larry Littlebird, it was not until 1999 that the real breakthrough occurred with *Smoke Signals.* The film, scripted by Sherman Alexie (Spokane/Coeur d'Alene) and directed by Chris Eyre (Cheyenne/Arapahoe), is the first successful film to have satisfied these basic requirements. Again we find Adam Beach (Anishinaabe) sharing the lead role as he pits his basketball brawn against the class wit, magnificently acted by Evan Adams (Coast Salish, British Columbia). Like its 1989 predecessor, *Powwow Highway,* in which Gary Farmer enacts a vision quest, the plot of *Smoke Signals* involves two comrades on the road searching for Beach's father—also played by Gary Farmer (Cayuga Nation).

In 2002 director Chris Eyre released yet another film, *Skins,* based on Adrian Louis's novel by that title. It explores the relationship between two men, a tribal cop and his alcoholic brother. Eyre told Delphine Redshirt: "*Skins* is not about assimilated Indians. This movie is about people who have spent decades and decades just surviving" (2002, 25). At this stage in history Chris Eyre has done for Indian film what Spike Lee has done for Black cinema, offering comic or serious treatments of racial conflict and issues of survival while using Native peoples as actors when the role calls for it instead of having white actors in red face.

Most of these films, while acted by tribally registered Indians, star male actors in male roles. Usually these men are partners: fugitives, tribal police, Indians on a quest. If a woman is featured, she assumes a subsidiary role: Pocahontas, the Indian maiden who reportedly saved the life of Captain John Smith; Mary McDonnell, the Sioux woman (but really a settler) who falls in love with Kevin Costner in *Dances with Wolves*. According to Jacqueline Kilpatrick, "In hundreds of films made during the last century, Indian women have been seen sacrificing themselves and their tribal communities for their white lovers" (1999, 152).

There is one film, not indexed in Kilpatrick's *Celluloid Indians*, in which a strong woman character takes charge of the narrative. *Lakota Woman*, produced by Turner TV in 1994, is based on the autobiography by Mary Crow Dog, coauthored with Richard Erdoes. It tells the story of a Sioux woman's struggle for selfhood during the second Battle of Wounded Knee in 1973. Starring Irene Bedard (*Smoke Signals*) the video focuses on Mary Crow Dog's early miseducation, her desire for sexual freedom, and her troubled relationship with AIM (American Indian Movement) leader Leonard Crow Dog.

Probably the most authentic achievement in Indian filmmaking for the twenty-first century is *Atanarjuat: The Fast Runner*, director Zacharias Kunuk's account of his nomadic childhood as a sub-Arctic Inuit. When Kunuk was nine his parents sent him to school in the village of Igloolik. There he learned English and learned to make videos, eventually filming a culture that had gone from 4,000 years of storytelling directly to filmmaking, having skipped the written language almost entirely. The film is absolutely stunning in its depiction of a frozen world where heroism is tested with a harshness that resembles Yellow Kidney's endured mutilation in *Fools Crow*.

We asked Welch about his own potential involvement with film, particularly whether a movie is to be made of *Fools Crow*, a film that would show what Native Americans were like before John Wayne. He answered that while almost all of his books have been optioned for film, a French filmmaker is especially interested in filming *The Heartsong of Charging Elk*. "We think it would be dynamite as a French movie. I like the French. I think they could make a good, historical movie about an Indian, set in Marseilles" ("Montana Interview"). We talked briefly about other Hollywood films containing fewer stereotypes, like *Buffalo Bill and the Indians*, directed by Robert Altman (1976), a movie that Welch enjoyed except that it made him feel "claustrophobic."

A few films that I would personally recommend are *The Black Robe* (Bruce Beresford, 1992), starkly set in the 1600s in eastern Canada; and

*Clear Cut* (Richard Bugiaski, 1992), a contemporary revenge film against rapers of the environment starring Graham Greene and the famous Indian old-timer, Floyd Red Crow Westerman. These and hundreds of other movies and videos about Indians are available. Viewers are encouraged to consult an Internet list or to review the Filmography section of *Celluloid Indians* (Kilpatrick 1999, 249–50) so they can make their own judgments about the positive and negative images of Hollywood's Indians.

Although Adam Beach, Graham Greene, Wes Studi, Floyd Red Crow Westerman and other non-Native counterparts—Richard Dix, Raquel Welch, Daniel Day-Lewis, Lou Diamond Phillips—have been playing Indians for quite some time, the crucial difference lies finally not in the actors but rather in the writers, directors, and producers who control the film. Welch believes that until Indians "get control of the back side of the camera" they will only be presenting the "white director's vision, Kevin Costner's vision" ("Wylie Tales: An Interview with James Welch" 1995, 2–3). Until more directors with the skills of Chris Eyre, Sherman Alexie, and Zacharias Kunuk are able to control their own narratives, we are in danger of getting more "Hollywood Indians," more Indian look-alikes who wear war paint to disguise their true identity.

# 3

# *Winter in the Blood*
# (1974)

*Winter in the Blood,* James Welch's first and most widely critiqued novel, was written when he was in his early thirties. In 1977, three years after its publication, the Modern Language Association of America held a seminar on *Winter in the Blood* at its annual convention. The literary discourse generated immediate interest in Welch's novel; it was followed in 1978 with the publication of six of the seminar papers plus two others in a Special Symposium issue of *American Indian Quarterly,* edited by Peter G. Beidler. These papers are individually cited in the text under the last name of the author, year (1978), and page number. Participants who attended the Discussion Session following the presentation of papers are named in the text when their identities are known but are not included in the formal Bibliography. All other related materials are listed alphabetically according to author under the *Winter in the Blood* section of the bibliography.

## NARRATIVE POINT OF VIEW

Point of view addresses the technical problem of how a story gets told. *A Glossary of Literary Terms* outlines the various ways an author presents his or her narrative (Abrams 1999, 231–36). In the first-person mode, the narrator, the "I," limits the experiences of the central character to the perceptions of that particular individual, whereas in the more complex, third-person point of view the narrator is outside the story, with the action performed by a person other than "I." Abrams further divides third-person narration into the omniscient or the limited points of view, each of which has subdivisions.

As readers approach Welch's novels they will raise certain questions about the narrative point of view: Is the story told in first person or third person? By a contemporary Indian or by a Plains Indian of the nineteenth century? With what tribe is the central character affiliated, if any? Does the narrator use his own voice or is there an outsider telling the story? Is the story told in a general way or is it tightened through its focus on the perceptions of a single he or she—what is known as the third-person omniscient point of view? (Abrams 1999, 232). Since Welch has never told the same story, his narrative perspective always differs.

While poetry and fiction often share similar themes, their narrative point of view is usually quite different. The poems in *Riding the Earthboy 40* (1971) are short and intense. They tend to use the personal "I" or the collective "we" as they record a goose biting Grandma's hand or a hawk strangling a mouse. They often create a setting, for example in "The Only Bar in Dixon," in which the men in the bar resist the temptation to take a "redhead" to Canada.

*Winter in the Blood* is preceded by an epigraph, or short introductory quotation, a technique that Welch also employs in The *Death of Jim Loney.* In *Winter in the Blood* the epigraph is a tightly structured nine-line segment, written in first person, from the title poem of Welch's own collection, *Riding the Earthboy 40*. He does not identify the epigraph, nor do any of the Symposium critics with the exception of Nora Baker Barry, who connects the poetic fragment to what she calls the novel's Gothic element, arguing that the epigraph helps to set the tone for the Ruin theme of the novel's beginning, with its gravestones and bleached logs (Barry 1978, 150).

The poem itself begins with the word *Earthboy* and ends, as does the segment, with the lines "Earthboy calls me from my dream:/Dirt is where the dreams must end" ([1971] 1997, 32). The word *Earthboys* also appears on the first page of Welch's first novel, marking the property and the graves of his former neighbors, although the house had been unoccupied for 20 years and nobody "by that name (or any other)" had been there (1). The reference to the dead Earthboys seems to be a signing off, a "burying" of the stage of Welch's creative life when poetry was paramount, and an entrance into the unexplored form of narrative fiction. When I suggested the Earthboy connection during the Montana Interview, he seemed amused:

"A lot of people ask me what I meant or if I meant this to be this particular way. But that's the first time I've heard this one. I think anybody's interpretation is as good as mine."

Because *Winter in the Blood* is Welch's first novel, it is not surprising that he unfolds the events from the perspective of the first person, this considered to be the least complex of narrative forms. But regardless of point of view, the author usually names his central character, at times in the title— as F. Scott Fitzgerald named Jay Gatsby or Mary Shelley named Victor Frankenstein. What distinguishes *Winter in the Blood* from almost every other novel of its time is the author's refusal to identify the person who tells the story. The "I" of *Winter in the Blood* is never mentioned by name, never given a title, even though the Earthboys, local residents, are negatively "named" on the first page. Even though Welch was a novice at writing fiction, he had created a point of view unusual to readers of contemporary fiction: the first-person narrator who remains unnamed throughout the book.

Welch's method of unfolding the events through an unnamed first person, while unusual, approximates the narrative method of Ralph Ellison's novel *Invisible Man* (1952). Ellison's narrator is an African American and therefore invisible to the dominant culture (Abrams 1999, 234). In the same vein, the narrator of *Winter in the Blood* is a nameless Indian and also "invisible." Welch's narrator, in unraveling his omitted or unnamed Blackfeet past, becomes "his story's first reader" (Eisenstein 1994, 14).

Although the ritual of naming is a central feature of Indian life, the "I" of *Winter in the Blood* is nameless, an Indian unable to acknowledge the personal and tribal foundations that might otherwise sustain him. He mentions the day he saw his father "peeing what he said was my name in the snow" (161), but he doesn't reveal what in this case is a mere illusion of a name, like a sand picture drawn at low tide. Elsewhere Welch again uses this absence of name quite consciously; following a barroom brawl in which he had helped rob a cowboy, he worries that someone "might have described me or given him my name"(54).

Almost all of Welch's critics refer to the protagonist's namelessness and have offered a variety of explanations for it. Nora Baker Barry, for example, believes that the namelessness gives the novel a "sense of willful non-being" (Barry 1978, 152), while A. LaVonne Ruoff suggests that the "anonymous narrator" may refer to the "traditional reluctance of the Blackfeet to tell their names for fear it will bring bad luck" (Ruoff "Alienation" 1978, 121, 1n). In identifying the unnamed narrator, Steven Tatum solves the problem, albeit awkwardly, by consistently referring to him as "Welch's 'I'." One amazon.com reader, troubled by the lack of name and by the novel in general, insisted on calling him "James" (Ruffino 2001). Welch himself has stated that he never named the character because "he didn't do anything significant enough to give him a name" (*American Audio Prose Library* 1985).

## ORAL AND WRITTEN SOURCES

Critics of *Winter in the Blood* have been anxious to place this extraordinary first novel within two literary traditions—European and Native American. Alan R. Velie contends that Welch was very much aware of Kurt Vonnegut, Philip Roth, Ishmael Reed, and other mainstream writers whose novels, like Welch's *Winter in the Blood,* were "fundamentally comic," although he also places Welch within the framework of the more serious "epiphany" style of Irish novelist James Joyce (Velie 1978, 142–44). Several critics compare Welch's novel to Ernest Hemingway's short story "Big Two-Hearted River." According to Louise Barnett, Hemingway's character, Nick Adams, is engaged in a "highly ritualized fishing trip" that serves as a foil for the narrator's unsuccessful fishing in *Winter in the Blood* (Barnett 1978, 124). Paul Eisenstein also connects Welch to Hemingway, making the excellent point that in Hemingway's collection, *In Our Time,* Euro-American readers are conscious of the omitted history of World War I because they already know it, whereas in *Winter in the Blood* Welch is working with a "mythic view of existence that becomes all but invisible when the history itself is marginalized" (Eisenstein 1994, 14). Sometimes the literary associations are unsupported, as in Charles G. Ballard's claim that the protagonist's walk through town carrying a purple teddy bear is an allusion to Mark Twain's *Huckleberry Finn*: "And just as Huck transported Jim the runaway slave on his raft, so the Indian narrator, in a more ridiculous way, carries the purple teddy bear in his arms" (Ballard 1991–92, 73).

More ethno-centered readings have focused on the protagonist of *Winter in the Blood* as a trickster–hero. As noted in Chapter 2, the animal trickster appears in many of the Blackfeet tales. The narrator's relationship with the animal characters Bird and Amos, as well as his generally antisocial behavior and his transformations from drunk to son to cow-saver suggest his trickster affiliation. The narrator's attachment to his grandfather, "Old Man," also connects him to Na'pi, the Blackfeet trickster.

Being a contemporary writer, Welch has been actively engaged in what some literary historians have called a Native American Cultural Renaissance sparked by the publication of N. Scott Momaday's novel, *House*

*Made of Dawn* ([1934] 1966). *Winter in the Blood* shares with *House Made of Dawn* an alienated protagonist, the structure of the journey, and the pattern of return. In both novels there is a dead brother whose absence must be recalled for spiritual regeneration to occur. One finds similar patterns of return and regeneration in Leslie Silko's *Ceremony* (1977) and Louise Erdrich's *Love Medicine* (1984). In addition, *Winter in the Blood* exhibits perhaps the major attribute of the Cultural Renaissance: the desire to recover the forgotten history of a people who have experienced what it means to be both Native and American, people who have identified with that experience through a process of recovery.

## STRUCTURE

Structure relates to the shape of a narrative, to its composition as an interconnected series of patterns. Structure is "the planned framework of a piece of literature," determined by features like repetitions, subdivisions, and total organization (Harmon and Holman 2000, 459). This definition, while accurate enough, applies primarily to European narrative. Here, I argue that the "planned framework" or structure in Welch's novels is grounded, first, in the characters' relationship to the natural/animal world, a concept analogous to *mitakuye oyasin* ("all are related"); and, second, in the pursuit of the vision quest, a tribal ritual that depends on departure and return. These primary considerations supercede but do not exclude more general concerns such as chapter divisions or repeated imagery.

### General Matters of Structure

In his overview of *Winter in the Blood* in *Understanding James Welch*, Ron McFarland notes its disruptive structure. "The transitions between sections are often abrupt and without logical or causal connection" (McFarland 2000, 61). McFarland attributes this abruptness to the picaresque or episodic nature of its structure. Like the classic picaro (Spanish for "rogue"), the protagonist relates his adventures in first person and shows a fragmented or satiric consciousness. McFarland cautions against applying this structure too strictly, however. "The unnamed protagonist of Welch's novel never approaches the lightheartedness or innocence often ascribed to the picaresque hero, nor does he exhibit the wit or cleverness often associated with this type" (McFarland 2000, 75).

Although McFarland's picaresque reading is a reasonable one, the explanation offered by Kathleen Sands is more imaginative. She argues that the actual narrative is "broken" to reflect the nameless narrator, for whom there is "no past, no present, and certainly no future, only the chaos of disconnected memories, desperate actions, and useless conversation" (Sands 1978, 97). Sands reinforces her pessimistic interpretation of structure with other considerations: the confused story of the dead ducks; the intermittent references to the death of the protagonist's father; the jarring appearance and disappearance of a character known as the airplane man. "As the narratives are broken, so is the man" (Sands 1978, 98). Only when he cleanses himself from the town and achieves a tribal identity is the narrator able to piece his story into "a painful acceptance of the present" (Sands 1978, 105).

The frame of *Winter in the Blood* hangs on a series of past memories, a fairly conventional device in modern fiction. Welch creates his narration through the voice of an anonymous Indian farmer, someone whose entire life had been spent coexisting with the earth, baling hay, and getting drunk, someone whose personal and tribal past remains on the periphery of his vision until almost the end of the novel. Welch moves his character back and forth in the narrative, often without transition, a method that possibly relates to his changeover from the freedom of individual poems to the constrictions of narrative form. The structure is wandering or circular, the wanderer taking on the characteristics of a man on a quest.

Structure in *Winter in the Blood* is also conveyed through repetition. The Earthboys' grave, which opens the novel, is parallel to the grandmother's grave, which closes it. The journeys to and from town at the beginning and the end make the novel "circular in form" (Welch, *American Audio Prose Library* 1985). The punctuated presence of certain repeated characters, like the airplane man and the Earthboy family, creates a structural framework, even though the characters themselves are secondary.

In terms of formal design, *Winter in the Blood* is divided into four parts and an epilogue, as if to suggest a five-part drama. These parts are composed of sections of varying and arbitrary length and seem to serve no particular purpose in terms of section division, since the narrative does not follow a chronological development but rather unfolds through memories and flashbacks. Welch couches his disjointed narrative within two specific structural conventions found in European literature—the epigraph and the epilogue, sections at the beginning and at the end of the work itself. These two forms, which originated with the ancient Greek poets, are usually ignored by Welch's critics, perhaps because they are so thoroughly embedded in Western literary tradition that they would detract from arguments supporting the novel's ethnicity or Indianness.

## The Quest

As mentioned previously, a concept of tremendous significance to the structure of Welch's fiction is the motif of the quest and its subsequent return. William W. Thackeray argues that the vision quest of the Native American should be viewed as distinctive, one that differs from the archetypal quest—myth found in most western mythologies—because of the status of animals and the meanings assigned to them within the Gros Ventre and Arapaho cultures. At the end of his essay he provides an intricate but imperfect chart of animal myths among the Gros Ventres as they relate to the vision quest. The DUCK, for instance, equals LIFE AND PURITY (Thackeray 1985, 63, emphasis in original). Thackeray stands on firmer ground when he abandons such symbolism for a more general cultural view of the novel: The narrator of *Winter in the Blood* should be examined within the context of the Arapaho vision quest instead of "in the medieval context of the Christian quest for the Holy Grail or the ancient quest of Oedipus for self-realization" (Thackeray 1985, 39).

In her essay on Anglo-Saxon themes and their occurrence in the American Indian folktale, Nora Baker Barry outlines the patterns of loss in Old English elegies: the Ruin theme, the Exile theme, the Last Survivor theme, and the Funeral theme (Barry 1978, 149–50). Each of these themes is present in *Winter in the Blood*, she argues, referring to several Blackfeet stories but giving her greatest attention to the Western model.

As a student of European literature Welch was surely aware of the significance of the quest motif in Anglo-Saxon and Medieval literature, although he modifies the European motifs by way of his grandmother's stories, his historical sources, and his own sensibilities. In his attempt to regain what had been lost, the farmer–hero appears to be conducting a mock-heroic quest, experiencing barroom battles rather than the more glamorous trysts of epic and romance convention.

Although Barry's list of stages in the Old English elegy helps to convey the ritualistic nature of the narrator's journey, the ritual must be read as part of the larger quest for ethnic wholeness. If Welch in fact had the English elegy in mind, he seems to be using it for satirical reasons. The protagonist's desire to reclaim the Cree woman, Agnes, is secondary to his desire for a tribal identity. Initially isolated from land, family, and culture, he perceives himself as being far from others in space, time, or relationship. Using a metaphor that dominates his fiction, Welch compares his "distance" to the flight of a bird: "I was as distant from myself as a hawk from the moon" (2). Although cultural heritage is represented through certain objects, like the grandmother's medicine pouch and the bird, it is only near the end of the novel, in his encounter with the grandfather, that he realizes his fundamentally Indian heritage and his place within it. The narrator's "reinterpretation of his tie to his ancestry places him in a world of rich history and belief and fills a previous cultural emptiness, thus making better sense of his world" (Teuton 2001, 646).

## PLOT DEVELOPMENT

Plot operates as a facilitator that joins the disparate parts into a coherent whole containing a beginning, a middle, and an end. The authors of *A Handbook to Literature* define *plot* as "an intelligent overview of action" (Harmon and Holman 2000, 394). They also contend that plot development enables a work of fiction to resolve the conflict among characters, characters being those individuals whose antagonisms form the basis of the plot. "Without conflict, *plot* hardly exists" (emphasis theirs, 361).

Welch recognized the necessity for developing plot through conflict or confrontation, something he did not need to do in his poetry. "My poems are about things," he said, "but they're not narrative enough to really be about things. So I got to thinking more in terms of narrative. I thought about short stories, I thought of nonfiction stories. I wanted to do a nonfiction piece about this. Then I got to thinking, who would be the kidnapper? And I started thinking in terms of characters and so on" ("Baltimore Interview").

Like many of his Indian contemporaries, Welch conveys the conflicts of plot by using a pattern of departure and return in which the central character goes on an adventure that involves his separation from the community and his inevitable reentry. *Winter in the Blood* begins with an unnamed Indian experiencing his first return from town with a swollen eye after having had a fight with a settler. "Coming home was not easy anymore," he thinks to himself (2). He is coming home to a disordered household: his mother, Teresa; a girlfriend, Agnes, whom he had earlier brought back from town; his grandmother, who hates Agnes because she is a Cree; and Lame Bull, a farm hand who wants to marry Teresa. Agnes is caught between two cultures: the town atmosphere, where she sees herself as sexually desirable, and her life at the ranch, where she sits all day with the grandmother and reads movie magazines, thinking she is Raquel Welch, possibly an ironic pun on the author's last name (Horton 1978, 133). After a short time in bored captivity Agnes runs off to town, stealing her lover's gun and his razor.

Distressed by his mother's remarriage to Lame Bull, the protagonist goes into the neighboring towns in search of Agnes. There he has sex with several women in an effort to achieve a sense of identity. The protagonist goes in and out of towns, in and out of bars, having one-night stands. He wanders from Malta to Harlem and later to Havre looking for Agnes, going to places that, according to Lois Welch, are not symbolic but were intended in the nineteenth century to help immigrants remember the stops on the railroad ("Montana Interview").

During the second homecoming the narrator goes to his grandfather's shack, where he experiences the process of personal and tribal discovery. Here Welch presents the most climactic moment of the novel, the moment of spiritual awareness when the protagonist sees at last the truth of Teresa's birth and of his own ancestry. This scene is followed by the protagonist's third return to the farm and his heroic struggle to save the cow who had caused his brother Mose's death by breaking away from the herd so many years before.

For many readers, the third homecoming creates the greatest confusion in following the plot. The narrator and his horse, Bird, after the visit to the grandfather, pass a graveyard. Coming back to the farm in the rain, they find a cow drowning in the mud. All of the last section, Chapter 41, is an action-filled battle against rain and muck. Like a mud-slinging rodeo or like a carousel ride gone berserk, the horse and the cow, the muck and the man are all related in one colossal action, in a graphic rendition of *mitakuye oyasin*.

Welch leaves the reader unprepared for so frenzied an ending, perhaps because he has withheld the facts about Mose's death until so late in the novel that the reader cannot make the immediate connection between horse and cow and Mose. Then too, in the last scene, there is a great deal of ambiguity in the protagonist's efforts to rescue the cow caught in a mud slick. Does the calf die? Does the cow die? Does the horse drop dead after saving or not saving the cow? Is his damaged knee permanently wounded by the rescue efforts? Other perplexed readers have asked similar questions. One critic finds the reference to the cow "unclear" (Davis 1986, 43, 13n); another, admitting to the same confusion, suggests that Welch's ambiguity in this and other instances is the author's way to "heighten the mysteries of just who the narrator was and who he is now" (Gish 1986, 52). Or, one might wonder, does the potential link between *Winter in the Blood* and earlier Blackfeet legends make questions of clarity and continuity beside the point? Having read the rescue scene many times without a sense of clear understanding, I asked James Welch in Baltimore about this and several other episodes in his novels that I found confusing. Smiling, he took the author–trickster position that his fiction is often ambiguous and that the reader should not expect definite answers.

The protagonist's recognition and resolution in the body of the text are followed by an epilogue in which the surviving family, grandfather Yellow Calf excluded, bury the unnamed grandmother. This epilogue is both profound and profane. It begins with the words "We buried the old lady the next day"—not the shaman or the medicine woman or the mystic but "the old lady," a disrespectful phrase that makes one seriously question Jack Davis's interpretation that she "imprints in the narrator's mind the undying spirit of oneness with the natural world and the sense of living beauty" (Davis 1986, 36).

The disrespect continues when the mourners discover that the casket is too large for the grave site. Lame Bull solves the problem by getting into the grave and jumping up and down on the casket, in an action that, like his stepson's rescue of the cow, seems to parody a rodeo. This outlandish act is followed by Lame Bull's disjointed elegy to the old lady, who was a "simple woman" and "not the best mother the world" but who "never gave anybody any crap" (175–76). During the haphazard ceremony Welch's "I" is inattentive as his mind wanders to his bad leg and to his Cree girlfriend. When he hears the surviving horse whinny, he thinks about the connection between that horse and Bird. The final sentence of *Winter in the Blood* is the final return: "I threw the pouch into the grave" (176).

This last scene has been called "vaudevillian" (Barry 1978, 156) or "carnivalesque" (Tatum 1990, 92). Still, it has some meaning. Lame Bull is "trying to do in ritual form something you do for someone who has died and whose total way of life and values are gone," claimed Carter Revard, a discussant at the MLA session (1978, 160).

## CHARACTER DEVELOPMENT

*Character(s)* is a term used to describe the person(s) who performs the action(s) of a fictional work. In most works there is one character who occupies the major role. The unnamed central character of *Winter in the Blood* is a farmer by trade, an earthboy. He drives a tractor, rakes hay, drives the herd from the grazing land each year with his brother as winter draws near. Closely identified with his family and the land, he consistently mourns the death of his father, First Raise, and of his brother, Mose. The central character is not James Welch, although, like Welch, he is an Indian, initially modeled on Welch's college roommate (Welch, *American Audio*

*Prose Library* 1985). Certainly, some of Welch's personality traits are discernable, such as his love of landscape and his sensitivity to smells and sounds. But the protagonist, despite the use of first person, is not Welch, who had spent most of his adult life in the city of Missoula and not on a ranch. Welch was married to his long-term and supportive wife, Lois, whereas his fictional character is unstable and unsatiated. The differences are vast, like the Plains.

## Names, Animals, and Character Development

The namelessness of Welch's "I" has posed a dilemma for readers trying to understand the narrator. So too, Welch's use of names or non-names is an important but often baffling aspect of character development. Louise K. Barnett suggests that both mother Teresa (the saint) and brother Mose (the leader of his people) connect these principal characters to the Judeo-Christian culture that conflicts with tribal life (Barnett 1978, 129, 7n).

Welch also obfuscates matters for the general reader by characterizing animals as near-humans, by naming them and giving them histories. Animal references appear with great consistency, either as metaphors or as genuine presences. Yellow Calf's back trembled "like the folded wings of a hawk" (159); The horse named Bird swelled his belly "like a bloated cow" (61); Indians were "driven 'like cows' to their reservation" (157); an Oldsmobile floated "like a duck" along the windy road (127). Welch fills the novel with birds or animals who actively participate in the action. Magpies signal warnings. Fish vacate the river. A pheasant flies from the tall grass. As one participant who attended the discussion following the MLA papers observed, animals in *Winter in the Blood* "function as a kind of emotional barometer" (1978, 163).

Although William W. Thackeray examines the prominence of the cow, the horse, and the duck in the novel, relating them and other animals to the mythology of Welch's ancestors, the Blackfeet and the Gros Ventre nations, the majority of Welch's critics do not argue for the structural or thematic importance of animals in Welch's fiction. Nor do they refer to the concept of *mitakuye oyasin* in this context.

The novel has a heroic horse named Bird. The bird—above all, the eagle—was a common religious symbol among the Blackfeet and among Indian nations in general, whereas the horse was believed to help the medicine man or shaman to fly through the air on his way to the afterlife (Sams and Carson 1988, 177). In Blackfeet mythology the horse was considered to be "the supernatural transformation of an elk," the animal whom the narrator's father dreams of hunting in Glacier Park (Thackeray 1985, 54; 58, 15n.) For Paula Gunn Allen, who attended the 1978 discussion session, the horse named Bird is a "symbol for the warrior Indian" (1978, 163). Bird is also obviously a tired old horse.

In a compassionate section that runs for several pages (144–146), Welch's "I" talks to Bird, addressing him as an "old machine," imagining what Bird must have felt when he was turned into a workhorse and was castrated to make him "less temperamental." He continues speaking into Bird's ear: "Only you can tell me how it felt." When he performs his heroic act of rescuing the cow at the end of the novel, the protagonist is quite literally looping horse and cow together in the rain, feeling the intensity of his wounded leg and the pain of Bird's death.

The duck called Amos is the other nonhuman central to Welch's technique of characterization. The narrator and his brother Mose have some pet ducks who drown in a tub. There is one survivor, a duck named Amos, who gets cooked for Christmas dinner. The narrator thinks a bobcat killed Amos until his mother admits that she is the one who slaughtered him. Teresa is brutal about the slaying: "One duck can't be smarter than another. They're like Indians" (17). Teresa's action seems to mimic the brutality of the Blackfeet tale "The Red-Eyed Duck," in which Old Man kills and roasts a number of innocent ducks, only to have them stolen by a coyote (Grinnell [1913]; 1926, 185–188).

Clearly there is something morally questionable about killing and eating the family pet, especially when the duck is commonly related to the Gros Ventre myth of creation (see Thackeray 1978, 51–52.) Amos, the original survivor, is a possible reference to "the myth of the morning star" and to the protagonist's "medicine or secret helper" (Ruoff "Alienation" 1978, 117). To speculate even further: when pronounced aloud Amos can be heard as "a/moose" or Mose, the narrator's dead brother. The sacrifice of Mose parallels the sacrifice of Amos the duck. The name Amos, incidentally, contains three of the four letters found in Mose. The reader can derive satisfaction simply from interpreting Welch's process of character naming.

Often Welch develops character, as in the case of the protagonist, by giving no name at all, thus creating a sense of emptiness or vacuum. The grave of Mose, the dead brother, is unnamed: "There was no headstone, no name, no dates. My brother" (143). The barmaid from Malta is nameless, suggesting that she is "insignificant" to the men who lust only after her body (Ruoff "Alienation" 1978, 116). The strange white man whom the narrator meets in town is also unnamed, known only as airplane man.

When he refers to his grandparents, the narrator clearly names his grandfather, Yellow Calf, although his grandmother is not specifically named. She is introduced as "the old lady, my grandmother" (5) and goes to her grave as "the old lady" (173). She is also identified as Teresa's mother and as the youngest wife of Chief Standing Bear, beautiful, with hair "shiny as the wing of a raven" (37). The narrator's unwillingness either to name this woman or to recognize the sexual relationship between her and Yellow Calf until the end of the novel affirms his lack of self-knowledge but also makes the truth of his full-blood ancestry more explosive when he learns it.

## Female Characters

Characters in Welch's novels are often developed through their relationships with animals. They are also revealed in the more customary Oedipal way: through the strained relationships between fathers and sons, between mothers and sons, through memory, in dreams. The tensions between the protagonist and the women in *Winter in the Blood* are an integral part of the character development.

Teresa, his mother, is a respected and propertied woman. We learn from the early pages of the novel that her first husband, First Raise, was a dreamer and a planner who died before he ever got to shoot an elk in Glacier Park. Welch's "I" resents his mother's remarriage to Lame Bull after his father's death, suspecting that the ranch worker is an opportunist who wants Teresa's property. Teresa is large and handsome, one of Welch's many female characters who, while not central to the plot, nonetheless performs as best supporting actress—a Gertrude to her son's troubled Hamlet. She is a Catholic but also an Indian, the product of two conflicting heritages. She lies to her son. She slaughters the pet duck for dinner, putting food on the table when First Raise could not. One critic calls Teresa powerful or "castrating" because she reverses the traditional Blackfeet female role by having a husband who is dependent on her (Ruoff "Alienation" 1978, 110–12).

In a stunning passage the narrator, awakening with a hangover, recalls a dream of his mother hanging from a belt and giving birth to Amos the duck. She is shouting a warning to the airplane man, who was "rolling in the manure of the coral, from time to time washing his great pecker in a tub of water" (52). Her newborn is a duck with shiny feathers and a bent leg, who is suddenly raised, "up and through a dull sun" (52). While recognizing the "strong oedipal overtones" of this dream, Ruoff contends that the dangling Teresa is related to the Blackfeet myth of the morning star, with Amos surviving and flying into the sun (Ruoff "Alienation" 1978, 117).

The dream reveals the protagonist's complicity in the death of Amos/ Mose; it is his belt from which Teresa, the conceiving mother, dangles in his dream. The man rolling in manure seems to be a sordid reminder of his dead father, frozen in the barrow pit, while the wet duck with the crooked leg is a complicated dream image suggesting the narrator's wounded knee, the flight from reality, Christian resurrection, and the eerie reincarnation of the slaughtered animal helper. This kind of surrealist passage is rare in *Winter in the Blood*. Generally Welch preferred a down-to-earth approach to characterization and theme. In writing *Winter in the Blood*, "I was just trying to be realistic," he told Kay Bonetti (*American Audio Prose Library* 1985).

The hostile mother, the departed father, the rejecting lover, the wounded son—the Freudian paradigm is clearly represented in the protagonist's dream of his mother and in his quest for identification with his first father. Yet as much as a psychoanalytic reading lends itself to the novel, one must be careful in using it because of the prime importance of the Native American extended family and the grandparents or the elders. The Freudian critic is asked to deal not only with his or her own assumptions of the primal family but also to enhance them through an awareness of Blackfeet ritual and storytelling. The feminist critic must be particularly careful to avoid a reading that distorts the historicity of the environment that Welch is creating. Harlem, Havre, and Malta are towns where women have very little economic power; they hang around bars looking for men to pay their way. The protagonist has sex with a tough woman named Malvina, then with a barmaid from Malta, and finally with a kind, overweight woman named Marlene, who picks him off the pavement after he has been beaten up by Agnes's brother. In each of the sexual escapades he takes risks. The women are hostile and "castrating" (Ruoff "Alienation" 1978, 116); the men are violent and crazy. Most of the sexual activity in town is dirty, disappointing, or downright degrading (e.g., he slaps Marlene when she asks for oral sex). In these brief encounters the protagonist is embarking on a quest for his essential wholeness, which he attempts but cannot achieve through drunken sexual adventures with the women he meets in bars or on the street. At times the distinctions among the women get blurred, as do the towns along Highway 2, which follows the railroad line.

Agnes, the best developed of the women characters after Teresa, is appalled when her lover tells her to settle down and learn shorthand because of the "demand for secretaries" (112). Agnes is a single Indian woman from off the reservation, living without financial support in a small Montana town. Secretarial school is not what she can afford or what she's after.

## Wanted Men

The protagonist's interaction with his mother, his grandparents, and the farm animals contrasts sharply with his journey into the white male settlers' world of bars, cars, and fistfights. Whereas on the ranch he works and has some authority, in town he becomes the victim of the settlers' hatred and of his own lust. When he goes into the town of Havre in search of his Cree girlfriend, he confronts a world far more alien than the one at home.

Within the town environment Welch presents a number of perfectly drawn male characters. One, an enigmatic white man, also nameless, is frequently referred to as "the man who had torn up his plane ticket" or, more simply, "the airplane man" (48, 51 ff.). The airplane man staggers in and out of the text like the inexplicable Log Lady in David Lynch's popular television series *Twin Peaks* (1990). He hounds his friend about going fishing, even though the narrator keeps telling him there aren't any fish in the river. He tries to get the narrator to drive him across the border into Canada in what sounds like an espionage intrigue. Then at one point the man with the airplane tickets vanishes, gone from the text like a vampire at dawn. Does the narrator forget him? Was he ever really there? What does he mean? One critic is emphatic about the nonmeaning of the "dis" man: He is "the radical extreme of disorientation, dislocation, distrust, disillusionment, and disgust" (Sands 1978, 99). In the Discussion Session after the MLA Convention papers, Gene Ruoff contends that "the significance of the airplane man would ultimately be that he doesn't mean anything; he is just there to reflect the reader's expectations of traditional form, which plays off against what Welch is actually doing" (1978, Discussion Session, 161). One wonders at this point what it is that Welch and his critics are actually doing.

Welch's "I" gets drunk, forgets things, gets beaten up, goes into tirades, has hallucinations. In his nightmares he sees ghosts, "wanted men with ape faces, cuffed sleeves, and blue hands" (52). In the bars he sees settlers who had once joked with First Raise, men who seemed "foreign" with their organized lives (40). There are some crisp, clean sketches of car salesmen, sporting goods salesmen, bartenders. In one crazy scene an old man in a diner drops dead, with his face in a bowl of oatmeal. The episodes that occur off the reservation are generally fragmented. They lead no-where except to the next bar. At times the drunken protagonist distorts his experiences in town and in bed, something the reader might expect when the narrative is told from first-person point of view (Murfin and Ray 1997, 291).

Only when he returns again to the farm is he able to piece together his broken character through his grandfather's revelation of the truth in which "a larger kind of vision, and value, is finally restored" (Eisenstein 1994, 13).

From a spiritual perspective the grandfather, Yellow Calf, is the novel's most important male character. Through him the protagonist, formerly blind to the truth, finally recognizes that Yellow Calf is his blood grand-father and not the half-breed, Doagie, as he had always thought. In a climactic moment that foreshadows the historical perspective of Welch's epic novel *Fools Crow* (1986), Yellow Calf tells his grandson about the winter of 1883–84, Starvation Winter, when the old woman, once the youngest wife of Blackfeet Chief Standing Bear, survives because an un-identified stranger hunts food for her. This "stranger" is Yellow Calf, the revered grandfather, who in the elegiac tradition is the Last Survivor, the shaman or wise man who preserves the Indian gift for communicating with animals as well as for guarding the truth about the grandmother (Barry 1978, 154).

As if in a vision, Welch's "I" imagines his ancestors trudging through the snow, feels their hunger, shares a journey "in the presence of ghosts, in wind that called forth the muttering tepees, the blowing snow, the white air of the horses' nostrils" (159). The horses in this passage call up the ancestral horses who struggled and perished during Starvation Winter when, the buffalo gone, the Blackfeet waited for promised rations that never came. "The bewildered Blackfeet, often plagued by smallpox too, starved gruesomely. In the Starvation Winter of 1883–84 an estimated six hundred died" (Farr 1984, 18). The white air blowing from the horses' nostrils unites the ancient horses to heroic Old Bird, the workhorse, and unites Bird to the disclosure about to occur.

In his own eyes, physically blind though they are, the grandfather sees himself as a representation of the circle that dominates Indian mythology: "To an old dog like myself, the only cycle begins with birth and ends with death. This is the only cycle I know" (158). His wisdom also links him to the trickster, who in some stories is "the father of the Indian people and a potent conductor of spiritual forces in the form of sacred dreams" (Nich-ols, 1).

At the supreme moment of awareness Bird breaks the silence: "Bird farted" (158). The animal talks back, as if to answer all of the terrible questions that his drunken master had posed to him on their ride: How does it feel to be saddled? How does it feel to be castrated? How does it felt to grow old and die? Bird already knows the truth that his master has repressed; "his 'corruption' [flatulence] provides the vehicle for the narrator's visionary insight into Yellow Calf's story" (Thackeray 1985, 55). Sean Teuton reads this extraordinary scene as the union of the sacred and the profane, what he calls "fart-wisdom" (Teuton 2001, 644). It is also the union between the named and the nameless, the animal and the human. All are related.

## THEMATIC ISSUES

A literary theme is a subject or idea that recurs in a piece of writing often enough to provide the work with a distinctive pattern, shape, or meaning. It is thought to be moral rather than unifying (Murfin and Ray 1997, 400). Although here at times I address the moral implications of theme, I generally use the term in a broader sense, as a way of incorporating certain integrated concepts or motifs into a reading of Welch's fiction. Thematic issues are not merely righteous statements imposed upon a text but, rather, underlying thoughts that result from the careful construction of detail within the novel itself. In Welch's fiction there are many different concepts that appear and reappear, with the themes of return, identity, and relationship giving his works their interrelated oneness but also their fundamental conflict and ambiguity.

As noted previously, Native Americans are far more likely than settlers to share the view that man is related to all other living creatures. In *Winter in the Blood* this theme of relationship takes on monumental proportions as the horse, the cow, the calf, the drowned ducks and other farm animals help to determine the fate of the protagonist and of his dead brother, Mose. By finally confronting his brother's death as part of the natural order, the central voice is able to establish an "aesthetic distance" that leads to his personal regeneration (Kunz 1978, 99).

When he returns to the ranch and learns about his grandmother's death, the protagonist is at last able to acknowledge the death of his brother, Mose, as if the two spirits were part of a great circle. The shards of character are pieced together in the presence of the elder or grandfather.

The title themes, winter and blood, are unifying devices. The narrator's father dies in the winter, his frozen body a memory preserved in his son's mind. His brother dies at the approach of winter as the boys are driving the cows from the grazing land. Winter represents distance, isolation, death, purification. In the larger communal framework of the novel, winter has a tribal resonance. "Winter is the time of old age. The snow on the ground is white, and so is the hair of elders," writes Chris Roberts, describing the symbolism used in Indian powwows (Roberts 1998, 99). The image of the elders is relevant to the old man or grandfather, Yellow Calf.

Blood has an even more obvious tribal meaning. The Bloods are a Canadian branch of the Blackfeet tribe. Although the historical information is often confusing because tribal locations shifted in the nineteenth century, the subdivisions outlined by William E. Farr offer clarification: "The Blackfeet people comprised four major, closely related tribes; "The Siksika or Blackfeet proper; the Kainah or Blood; the Northern Pikuni or Northern Piegan; the Southern Pikuni or Southern Piegan" (Farr 1984, 4). Welch specifically mentioned the Bloods in the Baltimore Interview. Thus the title *Winter in the Blood* probably refers to Starvation Winter and to the Blood or Blackfeet identification.

Blood also conveys an ominous meaning. Like winter, blood suggests death; Mose's broken body and the slaughter of Amos the duck convey this connotation. But the flowing of blood is also a revelation. The truth of the narrator's ancestry comes to him as if through the old man's "blood in my veins" (160). Blood in this aspect becomes like DNA, the source of communication between the generations. It's as if "the narrator has experienced a sort of blood transfusion" (McFarland 2000, 67). Or, to quote the pun that concludes A. LaVonne Ruoff's essay on the feminine principle: "The winter in his blood has thawed" (Ruoff "Alienation" 1978, 121).

A final theme is the preservation of Plains culture, really and symbolically rendered through the use of the medicine pouch and implicit in both the winter and the blood motifs. The medicine pouch or sacred bundle is a prominent feature in *Fools Crow*, whereas in *The Indian Lawyer* it serves as a memory of the past.

The pouch is in the possession of the protagonist's unnamed grandmother [Red Paint Woman], who had escaped the Marias Massacre and is a sacred elder a century old when she dies. In a burial ritual part Christian, part Indian, part haphazard, the grandson ends the mock ceremony by throwing his grandmother's medicine pouch into the open grave. This act is in keeping with Blackfeet burial practices, as evidenced by a photograph reprinted in *The Reservation Blackfeet, 1882–1945* that shows a traditional burial site. The text states: "Beloved possessions which accompanied a body in burial now came to include not just a familiar teepee rest, but a rocking chair as well" (Farr 1984, 36). The grandmother, the earth, the pouch, the shroud: All are related in life and death. The "I" (the I/ndian) throws her pouch into the grave for the final return; body and medicine return to the earth from which they came.

## STYLE AND LITERARY DEVICES

*Style* is an elusive term that presupposes a particular way of writing by a particular writer in either an individual novel or, more generally, as a common denominator in a writer's works. Stylistic elements would include word choice, sentence structure, rhythm, figures of speech, and the manner in which one's writing style echoes that of a former author. M. H. Abrams offers the conventional examples of Shakespearean style or Miltonic patterns (1999, 203–05). Style, as it is discussed by critics of contemporary Indian literature, would include an attention to written influences—in Welch's case Hemingway looms large—but also to a consideration of oral tradition and precolonialist language. As a trained poet, Welch is very close in some passages to the oral rhythms of the Blackfeet, even though he does not speak the language.

Welch's style is often earthy or crude or comic. Welch told me he loves Indian humor, giving the example of Sherman Alexie, author of *The Lone Ranger and Tonto Fistfight in Heaven* (1993), as a writer who "takes Indian literature in a slightly different direction. There's more humor and he even laughs at Indians, which I think is really good, because you need to laugh at yourselves. If you take yourselves too seriously, I think you really develop an image that only represents one side of the Indian personality" ("Baltimore Interview").

The comedic elements of Welch's first novel are peculiar to that book, however, and cannot be traced throughout his fiction. Although Welch admits to humorous elements in *Winter in the Blood*, he finds his later fiction to have "increasingly less humor," a claim verified by the immoderate gloom of his second novel, *The Death of Jim Loney*. Welch was unable to explain the discrepancy between what he writes and how he feels. "I don't know why. Socially I can be funny. I enjoy being with people who are having fun, especially Indian people. I love the humor, the banter, the teasing kind of quality that Indians have" ("Baltimore Interview").

Alan R. Velie rightly claims that scatology contributes to the comic effect. The word *scatology* refers to literature that focuses on obscene or excremental materials, as in the works of Faulkner or Chaucer. The first sentence of *Winter in the Blood* establishes the scatological style: The narrator "took a leak" while watching a mare and her colt walk from the hot grass into the shade (Velie 1978, 143). There are many other examples of this style. Bird pees while smelling the sage (160). Agnes's brother Dougie "peed" in a urinal (43). The narrator "peed" in Malvina's bathroom (84). In the bar in Malta he tends bar while the bartender leaves to "bleed my lizard" (57). At a bar in Havre we learn that the regular bartender is out because of "woman troubles," a polite reference to menstruation (91).

Welch's attention to physical realities like urination culminates in the notorious moment when, during the vision with the grandfather, "Bird farted" (158). In his literal explosion, the horse character "speaks" his relationship to his master just as the raven and the bear and the wolverine in Blackfeet folk tales spoke to Old Man and that they speak in Welch's magical novel *Fools Crow*. Although Welch has admitted to his desire to shock the tourists, these earthy details are not only part of his concept of characterization but also a graphic rendering of the language of Northern Montana.

The style in *Winter in the Blood* is varied. Welch has the uncanny ability to convey genuine speech patterns. His protagonist speaks to himself, thinks to himself, sometimes in a parody of heroic convention, sometimes in a convincing expression of sorrow, loss, or remorse. In a mocking treatment of conventional heroism, the flailing, cursing Indian who tries to save the cow in the final episode reduces himself and his nation to a simple phrase: "damn idiots, damn Indians" (169). But when he remembers his brother, one senses that an Indian brave has died in battle. He stands over the body, repeating the phrase "What use?" He gets no answer: "not the body in the road, not the hawk in the sky or the beetle in the earth; no one answered" (146). In this lamentation one hears the style of the poet turned novelist, especially through the repetition of the words "What use," words he futilely whispers to the wind and the clouds. The poetic style, enhanced by the absence of animals in earth and sky, perfectly captures the unnamed narrator's emotions as he releases his repressed memory of Mose's death.

## SETTING

M. H. Abrams defines *setting* as "the general locale, historical time, and social circumstances in which its action occurs" (1999, 284). Setting would include such considerations as racial distribution, climate, work environment, and many other associated factors. Montana provides the setting for all of Welch's nonfiction and for his first four novels. The fifth, *The*

*Heartsong of Charging Elk,* takes place in southern France with flashbacks to the Black Hills of South Dakota, the sacred grounds of the Sioux.

The Montana in *Winter in the Blood* is a world of smells and sounds, a sensual place. Welch loves to tell his interviewers the same basic story:

> Most people, when they come along Highway 2, through the Dakotas and through Eastern Montana, they always tell me that they drove like hell to get through that prairie so they could reach the mountains. So I got this idea of 'kidnapping' a carload of tourists, 'hijacking' them and taking them around, making them look at things, making them smell things—a pheasant in the evening, alfalfa, fresh manure in the coral at five o'clock in the morning, how sweet it smells. All of these sensual things. I didn't realize what an amazing world that is and not something we drive like hell to get through." ("Montana Interview")

Welch sets *Winter in the Blood* in the immediate sensuality of rural Montana, in the huge space of land that is the Gros Ventre–Assiniboine Fort Belknap reservation. The setting shifts from field to farmhouse to town; from on and off the reservation; from Malta to Harlem to Havre, towns in the Milk River Valley along Route 2. There is also a subsetting that encompasses the historical journey of Standing Bear's people from northwestern to north central Montana along the Marias River during the Starvation Winter of 1883–1884.

Many readers have the notion that an Indian reservation is a confined space. This is in a sense correct, since before the expanded settler invasion onto Blackfeet land in the 1850s there were no fences or road markers or property lines that kept Indians locked away. Still, it is important to recognize that in the reservation setting of *Winter in the Blood* the territory is vast. The confinement of the reservation is based on the hardships of economic and social conditions as much as it is on the limitations of geographical space. The border towns, while they too are confined, offer a break from the demands of farm labor. David Miller, a professor from Duke University who grew up in Harlem, Montana, rejects a theoretical or symbolic reading of setting of the novel. "I know a lot of those people. The bars exist. The novel is basically a portrait of existence on that parched piece of land in Montana. Like a very fine photograph, it is not only very realistic but also suggests the shapes in the background, the shadows" (Miller 1978, Discussion Session, 161). In the last section of this chapter I

further examine the background and shadows of *Winter in the Blood*, looking at the "piece of land" so fundamental to ecological criticism.

## ALTERNATIVE READING: ECOLOGICAL CRITICISM

Ecological criticism is a method of examining a literary work from the
perspective of its environment or landscape. It is also called "green studies." Rachel Carson's widely read books *The Silent Spring* (1962) and *The
Edge of the Sea* (1965) helped to stimulate a renewed interest in environmental issues such as water pollution and air pollution (McKusick 2000,
12). Although the term *ecocriticism* was first used by William Rueckert in
a 1978 essay "Literature and Ecology: An Experiment in Ecocriticism," it
did not become a recognized tool for literary critique until at least 10 years
later (Barry 2002, 249). Ecocriticism rarely shows up in theoretical texts
defining deconstruction, structuralism, Lacanian theory, and other more
abstract investigations of literature. It is not indexed in the more prestigious dictionaries of critical theory, like *The Johns Guide to Literary Theory
and Criticism*. Eco-practitioners are more likely to seek tenure at western
rather than at eastern universities, from places like the University of Nebraska rather than from the University of Pennsylvania.

In its early stages, ecocriticism was concerned with the themes of wilderness and nature, especially as these themes appear in the works of
American transcendentalist writers Henry David Thoreau (1817–1862);
Ralph Waldo Emerson (1803–1882); and Margaret Fuller (1810–1850) (see
Barry 2002, 249). This method of analysis can be applied, however, to any
work in which the setting is not a mere symbol for the character's mood
but an intrinsic element of the literary product, and in which style is not
simply an arrangement of words but a reflection of the rhythm of the
landscape. One writer claims that if a work of fiction or nonfiction involves environmental details, it is "automatically a part of this new literary territory known as 'eco-lit'" (Hunter 1992, 1).

Although both James McKusick and Peter Barry examine the nature
literature of Emerson, Thoreau, and other writers, using an ecological approach, only McKusick mentions Native Americans. Unfortunately, he
tends to imitate Thoreau in viewing Indians as objects in nature rather
than as interpreters of their own environment. He cites Thoreau's famous
description of the Maine woods: "Such is the home of the moose, the bear,
the caribou, the wolf, the beaver, and the Indian" (Thoreau, cited in
McKusick 2000, 166). McKusick claims that Thoreau's placement of the
Indian in this list "is not intended to denigrate these indigenous inhabi-

tants but rather to acknowledge their status as wild denizens of the forest, at home in their ancestral dwelling place" (McKusick 2000, 166). Yet Thoreau's apparent romanticization of the Indian reflects the popular belief in a Noble Savage, an aborigine who lived, untouched and uncontaminated, in a natural world. In his description Thoreau has assumed the privileged position of writer–observer. He admires the Indian, wants to eat wild berries like him, but never assumes a comparable consciousness. His desire to see Indians put into national parks where they can hunt and practice their traditions "without outside interference" (Thoreau, cited in McKusick 2000, 168) is in effect an argument for the reservation system. Although Thoreau's (and McKusick's) motives are sympathetic enough, they never anticipate what will happen when the settler wants those hunting grounds for himself.

Throughout this chapter we have talked about the Indian, the land, the muck, the barrow pit, the people and animals caught in the cycle of life and death. Perceived negatively, nature is incapable of retrieving a past that had already been destroyed a century before—in the vanishing of the buffalo, in the hunger of the people, in the defeat of Standing Bear, in the coercive placement of the Blackfeet and the Gros Ventre nations onto reservations.

Welch presents a number of clues to support a pessimistic ecological reading. The novel opens starkly, with gravestones, burned weeds, and an abandoned cabin that has become a "bare gray skeleton" (1). For an ecocritic these are not symbols of the character's psyche; rather, they convey the actual land that opens itself to the homecoming. The fish have disappeared from the "milky" river located downstream from a defunct sugar beet factory. Despite efforts by the government to replenish the waters, the fish have not returned. A cultural critic might relate the vanishing fish to the Blackfeet and Gros Ventre belief that fish were "unclean" or "taboo," while an ecological critic would claim that the fish can no longer live in a contaminated environment (see Thackeray 1985, 45, for both perspectives).

There are other negative environmental clues. Teresa hears a "sonic boom [that] rattled the shed door, then died in the distance" (20). The towns are dirty, not the dirt from the fields but "the invisible kind that coats a man who has been to town" (132).

The sinister environment has even invaded the grandfather's sanctuary. On an early visit the narrator is told that the deer are speaking to Yellow Calf of their unhappiness. "They know what a bad time it is. They can tell by the moon when the world is cockeyed" (68). Welch repeats *cockeyed* two more times (68, 69). He is so insistent with the use of the word that one is tempted to suspect a few puns—the barnyard animal, the grandfather's blindness, the male organ. Still, the word "cockeyed" is best read as a slang term meaning "slanted or twisted awry" (*Webster's New International Dictionary*). There is no longer a balance among ecosystems. The natural world is slanted. The grandfather says that at times he needs to "lean into the wind to stand straight" (69). As a symbiotic part of a "cockeyed earth," Yellow Calf's habitat could hardly represent the "uncontaminated world of natural process and harmony" that one reader attributes to it (Barnett 1978, 127).

Although very few critics of *Winter in the Blood* have commented on its numerous references to urination, an ecocentric reading might suggest that Welch's consistent openness towards natural functions is another way of placing his characters within the context of the landscape, of leaning into the wind. From the first "leak" in the first sentence, urine connects the narrator to the horse and to all other animals. Only humans living in a crowded, postindustrial environment would have the need for networks of sewers, sanitation systems, and portable toilets. William W. Farr gives convincing evidence, through text and photographs, of the ways in which required schooling, shorn hair, and the denial of Native languages were only a few of the physical restrictions placed on Indians in their transition from a free to a "civilized" culture.

The majority of Welch's critics interpret the ending of the novel as a positive affirmation of the narrator's quest for tribal personal and tribal identity. Robert M. Nelson, for example, maintains that the distance referred to throughout *Winter in the Blood* is the distance from the landscape, and that the return to the land of his grandfather suggests the potential for healing (Nelson 1993). Christopher Norden finds in certain works by contemporary Indian novelists, including *Winter in the Blood*, the possibility of reviving the meaningful relationships between man and his environment that resonate in the oral tradition. If the landscape is to be restored, he argues, then there must be a spiritual restoration as well. We must give back to nature what we have taken, through the aid of ritual (Norden 1994, 94–106).

There is perhaps another important link between the literature of ecology and its critique, one suggested by Stephen Tatum, who observes that the narrator of *Winter in the Blood*, in exploring his past for remnants or fossils of history, performs the tasks of gravedigger or archeologist (1990, 75). It seems that in like manner, the ecological critic performs the task of mining the text for environmental evidence, often uncovering either fossils of plants that have nurtured the soil or remnants of industrial debris that have poisoned the landscape. Viewed negatively, the planet is on the brink of collapse. Viewed positively, the environmental elements of *Winter in the Blood* help the central voice reclaim his place in the Milk River Valley, where all are related and the good winds prevail.

# 4

# *The Death of Jim Loney* (1979)

---

*The Death of Jim Loney* begins with an epigraph from Malcolm Lowry's novel *Under the Volcano,* which was published five years earlier. An epigraph is a literary convention that functions as an introduction; it is usually a quotation that appears prior to the beginning of a book, a chapter, or a section. If one reads Welch's title correctly, the novel actually begins not with the epigraph but with the title itself. The death of Jim Loney is announced before the novel begins—before the epigraph or the first word or the first page. The author thus eliminates a surprise ending. Other writers have used this technique before; one sees the death of the central character forewarned in classic literary works like Willa Cather's *Death Comes for the Archbishop* ([1927] 1990) and Arthur Miller's *Death of a Salesman* ([1949] 1998).

The opening citation from *Under the Volcano,* as well as the use of the literary technique of the epigraph, establish Welch as a writer indebted to European tradition. It also suggests that Jim Loney and Geoffrey Firmin, Lowry's protagonist, have something in common, as indeed they do. Both men are alienated and perceive themselves as failures. Both wander from bar to bar looking for consolation in alcohol. Both meet their deaths within the confinement of the narrative. It is interesting that both novelists were poets, although Lowry's poetry was not published until 1992, almost 20 years after his death.

## NARRATIVE POINT OF VIEW

Jim Loney's story is told by a third-person omniscient narrator, with the point of view focused on Jim Loney but capable of taking in other viewpoints. It is surprising that Ron McFarland, so acute otherwise in his reading of Welch, should confuse point of view in his chapter on *The Death of Jim Loney:* "Welch alters his narrative viewpoint from third-person limited in *Winter in the Blood* . . . to third-person omniscient in *The Death of Jim Loney.* . . ." (McFarland 2000, 92). As mentioned in chapter 3, the narrator of *Winter in the Blood* is a nameless "I," representing first-person point of view.

In Welch's second novel the protagonist is named immediately, first in the title and then in the text. The first word is "Loney": "Loney watched the muddy boys banging against each other" (1). The narrator is thus immediately given a name, unlike the unnamed Indian of *Winter in the Blood* whose story is recorded in his own voice. Loney "watched" the conflict, in this case a struggle among football players but later, in his own tragic game, a battle among himself, Myron Pretty Weasel, and a bear. As he observes the football game in the rain, he thinks about a passage from the Bible in which the man who has breath is of no account. While the lack of breath may relate to his team's losing performance, it also is another indicator of the hero's death and of the "crumbling of the house of Jacob" in a verse from Isaiah 2:22 (McFarland 2000, 89).

Loney "watched." Loney "thought." Welch, by using the third-person omniscient point of view, is able to enter the mind of his subject, capturing its confused patterns. This weaving from outside to inside, from thought to action, is characteristic of the narrative technique of all Welch's fiction.

*The Death of Jim Loney* begins mysteriously. Who are the "muddy boys"? Why does Loney recall the Biblical passage rejecting life and breath? Further reading reveals that he is watching a football game in the rain. His mind is blurred, "muddy" like the football players. It is possible that in using the word *muddy*, Welch is predicting the point of view of his central character while introducing a major theme, the plight of the half-blood, the Indian who is both Native and settler, both red and white.

## PLOT DEVELOPMENT

*The Death of Jim Loney* is divided into three parts. In the first section the reader overhears Loney's guarded conversation with Russell, an Indian bartender, following the football game. The scene then shifts to Jim's relationship with Rhea, a blonde from Texas who teaches in the local high school. Part 2 again begins in a bar; it entails a drunken fight between a white and an Indian. Then Jim's sister, Kate, arrives from Washington, DC, hoping to change his life. This section ends with Loney killing his hunting partner, Myron Pretty Weasel. In the third and final section Loney, after a heated encounter with his father, returns to the reservation, where he is shot. In each of his relationships Loney is beaten, a victim of the circumstances that surround his life.

Plot development in Welch's second novel is less fragmented than it is in *Winter in the Blood*, for several reasons. First, Welch confines most of the action to only two locations. Most of the action occurs in the small town of Harlem, just off the Gros Ventre reservation of northern Montana near the Canadian border; the death scene culminates in the Little Rockies, the mountain range on the perimeter of the reservation. Second, the plot is cohesively developed through a series of vivid scenes or episodes, more or less chronological, held together by the main character's acceptance or denial of relationship and by his dreams of a lost Indian mother. Third, by announcing Jim Loney's death in the title, Welch constructs a plot that moves inevitably forward, to an inescapable death. Although he is central to the plot, Jim is often seen as outside of it, a person unwilling to perform the actions that would change his fate and perhaps save his skin.

The plot ends as it begins, in the mind of its protagonist, in his "tangly brain," as he watches his body clock stopping, like the clock had stopped in the opening football game. Welch is here recalling the cyclical nature of Native American literature, with the end, like some dark bird, circling back to the beginning as Loney, the alienated Indian, comes home to die.

## STRUCTURE

### The Quest

Like *Winter in the Blood*, so *The Death of Jim Loney* is structured around a series of quests. First is the quest for personal and team victory. Jim's achievement as a basketball player has long since passed, his team photograph a memory in the display case at Harlem high school. Victory in regional sports might seem insignificant to European readers but is a key element in Indian culture, with basketball being the most typical opportunity for heroism. The football strategy that emerges in the opening scene involves running for a touchdown instead of kicking for extra points. The strategy is not successful; a victory is against all odds. Jim's team loses, a loss that foreshadows his own defeat, not only when he runs at the end of the novel but throughout the novel's entire development.

A second quest centers on the two women, his lover and his sister, who attempt to rescue Jim from his drunken and unheroic existence. Their struggle to win him over and take him away is more subtle than the barroom brawl that opens the second chapter. Still, they pursue their mission to save their man until each woman abandons her impossible quest and goes away without him.

Although the narrative structure clearly echoes the traditional Blackfeet theme of the vision quest, Welch alters or inverts the theme to emphasize his protagonist's estrangement from his Blackfeet heritage. Jim Loney is the nonhero, distanced from the past, dissatisfied with the present, and seeking his death in a wasteland or Shadowland. His quest climaxes in the shooting of Myron Pretty Weasel, the high school friend and hunting companion whom he presumably mistakes for a bear. Again Welch reverses the structure of traditional Indian narratives, in which the hunter kills the bear or antelope or buffalo, bringing food to his tribe and glory to himself (Grinnell [1892] 1962, 227–41).

After he kills Pretty Weasel, it is Jim who becomes the hunted animal, the victim. At the end of the novel, betrayed by his hated white father, Loney comes into the rifle sight of Doore, a reservation policeman who is by now engaged in his own personal quest—to track Loney down and kill him. Like a hunted animal or a great bird, Jim Loney plunges to his death, thus fulfilling the prophesy announced in the title. Some critics—Kathleen Sands, for example—interpret the structure of the novel as ending positively, in the completion of the vision quest; Loney's death is a form of "spiritual renewal" in which he returns to the reservation and "finally takes control, makes decisions, behaves deliberately and effectively" (Sands 1986, 132; 131). It seems questionable to grant so positive an evaluation to Loney's lonely death.

## Animals

Animals, their real and symbolic presence, provide an obvious structural element in *The Death of Jim Loney.* Welch's ironic application of the Sioux concept of *mitakuye oyasin* ("all are related") is essential to an understanding of his second and darkest novel. Although animals play a key role, they have an altogether different function from the traditional animal helpers of Blackfeet culture. They do not, like the raven, share in ceremonies or sacred functions. They do not, like the buffalo, enable the

tribe to "transcend[s] temporality" through myths of the origins of creation and of death (Campbell 1991, 98). Constructed outside of a tribal
context, the animals in *The Death of Jim Loney* are rarely sources of inspi-
ration. Rather, they are frequent referents to such themes as alienation,
separation, darkness, the hunt, and death.

Images of the horse, the bird, and the dog dominate the novel. The
epigraph from Malcolm Lowry's *Under the Volcano* is a light, rhythmic
praise song to a horse: "Ah, to have a horse, and gallop away, singing."
Throughout Lowry's novel a mysterious horse continuously recurs, once
on a road where a Mexican Indian lies dying. Yet except for a football
player on the first page who runs like a "regular horse," there are no lyrical
stallions in *The Death of Jim Loney*, suggesting that contemporary Indian
life is disassociated from the historic grandeur of the past, when horse
and rider were one. As he approaches the canyon to die, Loney sees a red
gas pump and a faded "flying red horse" (167). Like most of the animal
symbols in the novel, the dilapidated Mobil horse is a sign of the white
encroachment on Indian life. The post-reservation world has become a
junkyard.

The bird is the figure who seems occasionally to represent Jim Loney's
brighter side, his potential spirituality. "Birds have a special association
with the circle, a form which has special connotations of power for the
Plains Indian" (Brown 1997, 32). The bird, in one form or another, is mentioned at least a dozen times in *The Death of Jim Loney*, frequently enough
for the reader to notice its structural importance. Often the figure appears
to have no symbolic meaning. At other times the bird is connected to
death, darkness, spirituality, or some other theme central to the novel.

In the opening football scene, the extra-point kicker dances "like a thin
bird" as he follows the circling holder (2). Through the coordination and
circularity of these images that precede the team's defeat, Welch seems to
offer the illusory hope of *mitakuye oyasin*. Usually, though, the bird is perceived in isolation and appears to be alcohol related. Jim notices his hand
trembling and compares it to the trembling of the bird who comes at night
(20). Night after night Jim sits at his table drinking wine, the ideas in his
head as "tangled as a bird's nest" (21), a mental image that is repeated on
the last page: His mind became "tangly" (179). Loney has constant visions
of a large dark bird with strong wings that seem to falter, as if doomed to
fall, but still remains in flight (20, 68, 104, ff,). Dreams pursue him "like
dark birds" (168). He also envisions his Gros Ventre mother, Eletra Calf
Looking, as a bird–spirit, a "dream that one wishes to forget" (119).

Welch's most conspicuous use of the bird occurs in the last sentence.

Jim, hunted and shot, falls from a rock; his final vision is of "the beating wings of a dark bird as it climbed to a distant place" (179). The word "distant" recalls the opening chapter of *Winter in the Blood*, in which Welch compares his unnamed character's distance from self to a hawk's distance from the moon (2). The coincident pattern of the dark bird rising and of Jim falling suggests that redemption is possible only through relatedness and that Jim, because of his own reactions to nature and culture, is doomed to eternal separation. Dexter Westrum contends that the bird is a positive image that signifies the "survival and fulfillment which comes about when the protagonist becomes aware of his own Indianness" (Westrum 1986, 139). Although Westrum skillfully connects the interrelated bird pattern, he does not, given the overall tone of despair in the novel, make an adequate case for Loney's ethnic or spiritual self-discovery.

The one animal that means a lot to Jim is a dog named Swipesy, a lowly descendent of the dogs bonded to the heroic Blackfeet past. Every Indian nation, from the Southwest to the Northern Plains, had dogs (Sams and Carson 1988, 93). Before horses came to Montana, dogs performed heavy labor for the tribes by pulling the travois or long cart (Grinnell [1892] 1962). A delightful Ojibwa story tells of a "little mystery animal" who could change sizes so that two lost Indians could ride home on the dog's back. The dog's bravery saved them from being eaten by a mad beast (Horne 1999).

Swipesy is incapable of such heroism. He is "very old and deaf" (12), past his prime. His lowly nature makes him more reminiscent of the tattletale mongrel in "Why Dogs Can't Talk" than of his more heroic ancestors (Wissler and Duvall, ([1908] 1995, 133). One cold day Jim finds Swipesy near an alley, his body broken, "frozen" in the mud (53). The dog cannot be lifted, so a boy from "out there" (54), from the reservation near the Little Rockies, a boy called Amos After Buffalo, lends Loney a knife to hack Swipesy's body from the ice.

The death of Swipesy serves several functions. First, it separates Loney from his only attachment to the relational world of animals. Second, it suggests Loney's tenuous link to the past and to the survival of the Blackfeet people, represented by Amos After Buffalo. Finally, the death of the mongrel Swipesy predicts the death of the half-breed Loney while looking back to *Winter in the Blood*—to the death of the narrator's father, found frozen in the barrow pits, and to the near-winter death of the narrator's brother, another boy named Amos. In each instance death by freezing provides a relational context for father/brother/son, for man/dog. At the end of the novel Jim, who has fled to the Little Rockies, feels the frost and the cold: "He had never been this cold" (174). About to die, he realizes that his legs and lungs are "frozen" (175).

Other canines are mentioned in *The Death of Jim Loney*. His lover, Rhea, compares him to a "dark greyhound" (12). The majority of references to dogs convey a dark or sinister impression, like the snarling hounds who overturn the garbage cans at the side of Jim's house—"turdhounds," Loney calls them (11). These destructive dogs, along with a score of other animals, contribute to an emerging animal pattern that includes a buffalo, a porcupine, a muskrat, a weasel, a lamb, a sheepdog, a wolf, a bobcat, a deer, a bear, and the soaring dark bird.

## CHARACTER DEVELOPMENT

Jim Loney is a character estranged from the land, from the natural world, and from his heritage. He is literally "Loney"—alone or a loner. A half-breed without heroic disposition, Jim drinks too much and works too little. In his alienation he can be included among the many dispossessed male characters who inhabit contemporary fiction and film: Mogie in Adrian C. Louis's novel *Skins* (1995); Jake Barnes in Ernest Hemingway's novel *The Sun Also Rises* (1926); Ben Sanderson in Mike Figgis's film *Leaving Las Vegas* (1995). Because he is alienated from the community and from a world of shared values, Loney, through most of the novel, lacks the interpersonal and communal connections essential to generate his spiritual growth or, for that matter, to save his life. Like the protagonist of *Winter in the Blood*, he experiences the "pain of loss, the blankness of solitude, the numbing encounter with death" (Tatum 1990, 78). Although Jim Loney fails in his efforts to resurrect the past or handle the present, his failure is not simply a personal problem but is part of the culture. "He is like many young Indians who had too much pressure placed on them to be successful" (*American Audio Prose Library* 1985).

Loney's character unfolds through his various inadequate relationships—with a local bartender; with his lover, Rhea; with his sister, Kate; with his Caucasian father, Ike; with Eletra, his Gros Ventre dream/mother; with his high school friend, Myron Pretty Weasel; with real and imaginary animals. His characters "live in the sour stink of bars, sustained by alcohol and the pathetic triumphs of courtship and fist fights" (Logan 1979, 54).

Jim's hatred of his father, Ike, is perhaps the dominant relational theme, for through it Welch emphasizes Jim's fragmentation, his broken humanity. Initially Jim had admired Ike for his skills in hunting and trapping. He had seen his father identify a bobcat print simply by examining the empty trap (121). But the two become estranged after Jim's mother leaves Ike, a man of small character. The two men, father and son, live in Harlem without speaking until one day Jim confronts him in his quest for the truth about his natural mother. In a violent outburst that precedes Jim's brush with the law, Ike gives his son a "perfect bird gun" (149). Jim takes the weapon and blows out the window of Ike's trailer, sending shards of glass into his father's face. Ike retaliates by telling the police about his son's killing of Pretty Weasel, a betrayal that Jim seems to have planned all along.

Jim and Rhea provide the major love interest in *The Death of Jim Loney*. They are attracted by their racial and cultural differences; she is a wealthy blonde from Texas who loves Jim's dark skin and his lack of sophistication. Jim's sister Kate, who is visiting Montana from Washington DC, is a contemporary Indian who has achieved where Jim has failed. Her Navajo squash blossom necklace and a her sheepskin coat compliment her dark beauty and call attention to her ethnicity. When she was younger the boys used to call her "Ice Woman" (111). While half Indian like her brother, Kate has become "careless of her clan identity" (Nelson 1993, 112). Superior and cultivated, a dark bird in her own right, she has flown to Montana to save her brother's skin and to rescue him from what she sees as his harmful habitat. Kate is a strong Indian woman, "single-minded and determined to succeed," Welch told one interviewer. "Indian men of authority were always ruled by the government. I think that maybe Indian men became too compromised. The women became impatient" (*American Audio Prose Library* 1985). Although both women try to take him away—Rhea to Seattle and Kate to the District of Columbia—Jim is determined enough to refuse both of them, sustained by memories of the past and by the comforting mother who frequents his dreams.

As Welch uses animals for structural reasons, he also incorporates them into the development of his characters. When describing the two women who try to redeem him, he frequently describes their resemblance to animals. Rhea is associated with a cat; she has eyes "as deep and as flat" as the eyes of a cat (67). Welch assigns the same metaphor to Jim's elegant sister, Kate; she is a "dark cat" (62). The cat of these comparisons, though presumably domesticated, evokes the image of the lynx and the mountain lion, larger, ferocious cats at one time found on the northern Plains. The simile of the cat suggests that both women are sleek and dangerous intruders who threaten Jim Loney's sanctuary.

Rhea is, according to William Logan, the most fully developed character in the novel. Logan is impressed by the way her "inner strength keeps evaporating into defensive southern coyness" (Logan 1979, 54). In the animal kingdom, a rhea is an ostrichlike bird from South America that is unable to fly (*The Concise Columbia Encyclopedia*). In a brilliantly ironic episode, Rhea and Jim are making love in the front seat of Rhea's station wagon. Rhea has her eyes closed and is smelling her lover's hair. When she opens them she witnesses "a deer through the rear window.... It stood broadside, its head turned directly toward the car" (15). The irony of this event is that while Jim, the half Indian, is rendered incapable of visionary experience, Rhea has been made witness to the sacred deer. This witnessing, her "best secret ever" (15), is her personal vision quest. It proves her ability to fly.

For the Sioux the deer represents the swiftness and the power of the female (Brown 1997, 109), an interpretation that can be applied to this provocative passage from *The Death of Jim Loney*. Through her vision Rhea becomes the deer and embraces its feminine spirituality. Her powerful vision may remind filmgoers of the sanctified deer in Michael Cimino's *The Deer Hunter* (1978) and in Michael Apted's *Thunderheart* (1992). In both films a deer emerges in the center of the screen. The deer is viewed in Cimino's film by Robert de Niro, who spots it through a rifle scope but does not shoot it. In Michael Apted's film *Thunderheart* Val Kilmer and Graham Greene spot a deer in their headlights, not once but twice, as the spirit of the deer leads them to the uranium site that is polluting the Sioux's drinking water. In both films the mystical deer remains undefiled by human interference and is merely seen, much as Rhea "sees" the deer during sexual intercourse.

Among the Oglala Sioux there is more ominous meaning for the deer. It is believed that a deer can change sexes and, in its doe form, it can emit a strong odor: "Through this perfume, the doe is aided in luring the young man away to his death" (Brown 1997, 20). Earlier in the day Jim had admired her perfume, which is a sexually ambivalent scent, "Charlie" (12). Rhea's vision occurs while she is smelling Loney's oily hair, which possibly connects their perfume to his death. It is unlikely that Welch had this particular Sioux belief in mind, any more than that he intended Jim's lover to be an allusion to Rhea, wife of Cronus, a Greek goddess associated with fertility (*The Concise Columbia Encyclopedia*). Still, such speculation is prompted by Welch's consistent interest in the naming process.

Jim's mother is a memory from the past. Often she appears to him in dreams as a raven or dark bird, perhaps an emissary from her Gros Ventre ancestors. The messenger–bird was a common figure in Blackfeet myth (McClintock [1968]; 1999, 481–84). At times his dream/mother is protec-

tive, while at times she is ominous. As he is dying he reconciles her ambiguity in an image of freedom, imagining a place "not on this earth"
where there would be "no lost sons, no mothers searching" (175). It is
through the vision of the mother that Welch "makes a fundamental and
important statement" about the need to affirm the power of the feminine
principle (Antell 1988, 217).

If Loney's relationship with women is unstable, his relationship with
men is fatal. Jim is initially responsible for the death of Myron Pretty
Weasel, whom he mistakes for a bear. Then Jim's father, Ike, tells the police
of Jim's whereabouts, becoming the prime mover in his son's death. Finally, it is the duty of three reservation cops to "flush" and kill him (170).

When I asked Welch in Baltimore if Jim Loney had deliberately murdered his hunting companion, he answered, "That's part of the ambiguity.
Loney takes full responsibility for killing Pretty Weasel and he goes on
the run, which implies that he must think that shooting him was more
than an accident. Because you can explain away an accident."

"And what about the bear? Do you have to be totally connected to
Blackfeet mythology to understand the bear?"

He answered, "No. What I tried to make clear is that there used to be
bear in that part of the country. But because the white people came in, the
settlers and so on, they eventually drove the bear out, killed them all out.
I guess the bear represented this completely unusual phenomenon. It dis-
combobulated Loney."

I was insistent. "But was it a bear or a vision of a bear? I just want all
these answers!"

Welch said, "I'm leaving that ambiguous. In his mind it was a bear"
("Baltimore Interview").

After the interview I checked some references about the meaning of the
bear in Indian folklore. Joseph Epes Brown notes the bear's dual nature,
duality being considered a bear trait among the Sioux. "When confronted
by a bear the Indian cannot be sure if the bear is a man in bear form or
vice versa. It is not surprising, therefore, to find that even the bear's soul
is thought to be special among the animals" (Brown 1997, 22). The bear,
who seeks honey or truth, represents "introspection" (Sams and Carson
1988, 57). The Blackfeet tell an intricate story of a young half-breed who
enters the den of a family of bears. The son, a bear-helper, takes pity on
the man and, with his father's aid, gives the man a knife and teaches him
the bear medicine (Wissler and Duvall [1908] 1995, 95–98). Joseph Campbell talks about the hunter's need to appease the bear who has been killed;
otherwise, primitive hunters would die of starvation (Campbell 1991, 93–

94). It was believed among the Blackfeet that a grizzly could bestow his power on a warrior, who would then "inspire fear in his enemies" (McClintock [1968] 1999, 353). Or, as one critic suggests, the bear shifts its shape from sacred animal to human during the moment the gun is fired (In-the-Woods 1991, 164–65).

Perhaps, then, the bear is an apparition who seems real when Jim scopes it with a rifle. Perhaps Jim, who has no bear medicine, forgets to appease the bear-spirit. The answer remains ambiguous. The death of Pretty Weasel, however, holds no uncertainties. The tribal police promptly respond to his death. Betrayed by his own father, pursued through the Little Rockies by three tribal cops, Loney is not likely to have received a fair trial under tribal law if he was captured, even though Pretty Weasel's death was probably accidental, a gamble with fate.

## SETTING

Like *Winter in the Blood, The Death of Jim Loney* is set along U.S. Route 2, the "Highline," a road that slices through the mass of land that is the Gros Ventre—Assiniboine Fort Belknap reservation. It is set in the present (the late 1970s) in the town of Harlem, Montana. The atmosphere of the novel is bleak and cold. The October sky is "smoky" (3). It is too rainy for Jim to do farm work. Then winter comes. Clothes freeze on the line. Swipsey freezes in the ice. Sunlight is rare. Rhea is bored by the flat landscape, broken only by the mountains south of the town.

The interior settings are mutually bleak. Jim's small apartment is "dark" (19, 23) and overcrowded with furniture. Ike Loney's trailer, located in a remote part of town, is sparsely furnished with a table, some benches, a few tiny cupboards, a bed, and a "cubicle" that houses a toilet and shower head (136). Cars smell like stale booze. The bars are next to empty.

Near the end of the novel, as Jim trudges through the icy streams during his futile escape, the setting shifts from the town to the reservation, from the stench of Harlem to the frigid and perilous open air. In this awesome outdoor environment the reader is overwhelmed by the austerity of Montana's Little Rockies, which provide a sharp backdrop for Jim's lonely figure, outlined on a mountain ledge and viewed through the sights of a rifle. He has "no real home in nature or in the plastic substitutes available to him" (Kiely 1979, 14). The natural world offers Jim Loney neither protection nor solace.

## THEMATIC ISSUES

Theme has been defined as the central idea of a literary work, for example, "the vanity of human wishes" (Harmon and Holman 2000, 518). In *The Death of Jim Loney* the major theme is the alienation of the contemporary American Indian from his past. There are also a number of subthemes, developed through a series of repeated metaphors: racial identity; alcohol; and gaming. All of the subthemes support the idea of Loney's alienation.

The theme of racial identity is central to the novel. Jim Loney is a mixed-blood or half-breed; in Harlem, Montana, "to live halfbreed is to be dead" (Thackeray 1986, 136). It is through Jim's choppy conversations with Russell, an Indian bartender, that the issue of racial identity is first introduced. "Skin you," Loney says. Russell, who never liked Loney, nonetheless responds, "Skin you too. . . . It was an Indian joke" (6). Although Welch does not bring the reader in on the joke, it presumably has to do with the pun on Redskin. Neither full-blooded Redskin nor a *Napikwan* or white man, Jim perceives himself as a half-breed, caught between two birthrights. While Rhea in her naiveté thinks he's lucky to have a double ancestry so he can be "Indian one day and white the next," Jim has a different concept. He'd rather be Indian or white. "Whichever, it would be nicer than being a half-breed" (14).

Loney's "aloneness" from the tribe is reiterated throughout the text. Although he thinks about Indians, he "never felt" like one (102). Caught between two parents, a white father and an Indian mother, Loney is the only one of Welch's central characters who is a half-breed, although the protagonist of *Winter in the Blood* learns of his full-blooded ancestry only near the end of the novel. Other Indian novelists have examined the psychological problems of the half-breed, for example, Thomas King in his 1989 novel *Medicine River* and Adrian C. Louis, in his deeply disturbing novel *Skins* (1995). The fact that both of these novels have been adapted into film is a testament to their thematic power.

The racial theme is also apparent in the Indian-European sexual interchange. Rhea likes Jim because he is dark. Again we have a familiar racial theme, the sexual attraction between Indian men and Caucasian women and vice versa, found in films such as *The Searchers* (1956) and *Billy Jack* (1971); in Thomas King's novel *Medicine River* (1989); and in Welch's novels, *The Indian Lawyer* and *The Heartsong of Charging Elk*. Rhea is similar to the white woman in *Medicine River;* although both women want to save their lovers, they "do not understand" how being of mixed blood creates "conflict" in the minds of their Indian men (Mackie 1998, 2).

A second theme in *The Death of Jim Loney* is a concern about alcohol and the breakdown of the Indian psyche. In presenting this theme Welch comes dangerously close, as he does in some of his poetry and in *Winter in the Blood*, to repeating the cliché of the drunken Indian gone mad from the white man's liquor. In Baltimore I raised this issue, remembering that in the poetry, written when he was younger, there are a lot of drunks: people in bars, people falling down out of trucks going home. One reviewer has commented that both *Winter in the Blood* and *The Death of Jim Loney* "depict a wailing, bleak, alcoholic morass of contemporary reservation existence; they are bitter and amused, without self-pity" (Hoagland 1990, 7). Welch's response was honest: "In some way that's part of the problem. The drunks are very visible. I think I was guilty of promoting that image myself" ("Baltimore Interview").

Loney's drinking habits connect the various episodes of the book, from the early bar scene with Russell to the final ride, where he flees the car holding a bottle of scotch and a shotgun (166). Often he is described sitting at his table drinking wine, his mind a blur. Rhea participates in Jim's binges, even desires them. She wants to get drunk and "pass out" like her friend, Colleen (134). Jim's white father is an alcoholic who goes to Kenny's bar downtown and sponges drinks (137). Clearly, not all of Welch's drunks are Indians.

A third theme, one that lends continuity to *The Death of Jim Loney* and that is also explored in the chapter on *The Indian Lawyer*, is the idea of the game or, by extension, gaming or gambling. Welch mentions sports in all of his novels, albeit briefly in *Winter in the Blood* and *The Heartsong of Charging Elk*. The game is one of the few areas where Jim is connected to his past. There is a long and respectable history of traditional Indian games: stick games, hand games, "hubbub," guessing games, dice. Usually these games involved gambling and were meant spiritually to imitate the wager between life and death (Bruchac and Bruchac, 2000). Gambling among Indian nations was "nearly universal and served to redistribute goods among tribal members and to reaffirm social ties" (Hill 2003, 47).

*The Death of Jim Loney* opens with a losing game of football, a failure which symbolizes his life. Life is a game and Loney is a loser. His loss parallels the loss of the local Harlem team against the Chinooks and, looking backward to the post–Civil War era, it parallels the greater loss of indigenous peoples defeated by the United States Cavalry.

Jim's and Russell's conversation in the bar is focused on the Harlem team's loss. The reader learns that although Jim had once been a small-town hero as a player for the Harlem basketball team, memories of high school victories are all that remain. Rhea first meets her lover when she sells him a ticket to a basketball game. Loney mistakenly thinks that Rhea's interest in him was sparked by his team's championship picture in the school trophy case. But it's Jim she is attracted to, not his local reputation as a player. "She hates basketball," Jim tells his sister Kate (68). Participation in high school athletics, while it may have brought a sense of solidarity for four short years, does little to improve Jim's life or the lives of Myron Pretty Weasel and other former teammates who remain on or near the reservation.

Welch describes the novel's actions in terms of game playing. In *The Death of Jim Loney* the hunt is a game, a sport in which both Pretty Weasel and Loney lose their lives without ceremony, in the absence of ritual. While he is on the run he thinks about the game of basketball. Doore, the tribal cop who shoots him, realizes that the "manhunt had been a game" (178).

While some Indian athletes are remembered in history, through the triumphs of Sitting Bull and Crazy Horse at the Battle of Little Bighorn and through the victory of Olympic medalist Jim Thorpe, too many contests end in defeat or oblivion. One painful example is the short life of venerated Lakota basketball player SuAnne Big Crow, who led the Lady Thorpes to an all-state championship in 1989 and who died in a car crash on the morning of February 9, 1992 at the age of 17. At her wake in the school gym, her teammates climbed a ladder and cut the hoop, piece by piece, then placed the broken hoop in her still hands. After her death SuAnne's mother established a club, Happy Town, on the Pine Ridge reservation in her honor (Giago 2000, 1–3). The tales of fallen Indian heroes, like Gary Smith's account of cirrhosis among players and their families, are unbearably sad (Smith 1992, 1–23). Such disasters have been counterpointed by stories of modern Indians who take a chance in other fields by getting advanced degrees in hydrology, chemistry, and research biology (Gibson 2002, 26–31).

The game of chance, an ancient tradition among Indians, has in recent years helped to revolutionize the Native American economy through the building of casinos, many of them boasting spas, four-star hotels, and luxurious accommodations. *Native Peoples* goes so far as to call the Indian casino the "new buffalo": "Like the buffalo, gaming funds have literally—in some cases—put food on Indian's tables, shelter over their heads, and clothing on their backs" (Smith 2002, 26). In Indian literature, though, gambling often tends to be a metaphor for an unlucky marriage or for other moments when "characters take the risk and suffer losses" (Stookey 1999, 122). Some Indians reportedly believe that losing at gambling reflects a flaw in character or spirit and is not simply bad luck (Hill 2003, 46). In Loney's Montana the average legalized casino amounts to little more than some slot machines in a gas station. And even there he would suffer losses. In the dark vision that envelops this book about Loney's death, he is just too unlucky to be a winner.

## STYLE AND LITERARY DEVICES

Welch's style in his second novel is cleaner and less poetic than in *Winter in the Blood*, presumably because having written his first novel, he is more closely identified with the form and with its predecessors, especially with Ernest Hemingway. Pronouns, verbs, objects: these simple stylistic formulas become standard in *The Death of Jim Loney*. The novel has been praised for its "economy of style and feeling" (Kiely 1979, 14). At times this directness of style is intentionally complicated, as in the opening sentence, where Loney "watched" the players but simultaneously "thought" about the passage from the Bible.

A more important stylistic change relates to point of view. In shifting from the first to the third-person point of view, Welch introduces characters who are intensely engaged in conversation. His use of dialog in *The Death of Jim Loney*, impressive in itself, is frequently interrupted by a thought that creates a flashback, as in the following example, in which Rhea asks him: "Do you think—would you like Seattle?" (44).

Instead of answering, Jim attempts to "remember" Seattle. He then "remembers" for more than half a page before responding, "It's surrounded by mountains" (44). By manipulating gaps in response between characters and by using a panoply of cognitive verbs—"remembered," "know," "felt," "thinking," "thought"—Welch skillfully fleshes out what is often stark dialog.

Almost every critic of Welch's second novel has noticed another stylistic technique, the use of the dream, a device that is introduced in *Winter in the Blood* and that can be found in his later novels, especially in *Fools Crow*, in which dream becomes vision. Like warrior to shaman, like patient to psychiatrist, so Loney tells the reader his dreams. At times there is a third party, a dark bird that may be "a vision sent by my mother's people" (105). Loney's longest dream, a private vision, is an apparition of a woman in a pink stucco church near a graveyard. She is wearing a shawl and wailing "the way Indian women wail for their lost ones" (33). Her son is "out there," she says (34), pointing to the Little Rockies. The dream/ woman, whose face seems "familiar" to him (34), is a fairly undisguised image of the protective mother, the one who in Jim's imagination foresees his death. Jim's eloquent commemoration of his mother appears to signify his attempt to connect with the spirituality of his Indian heritage. The dream image is overridden by other, far coarser references, as in the metaphor that his life is "a real dream made of shit" (119). It is this "real dream" that becomes more and more inevitable as Loney moves towards his fateful, dreamless death.

## AN EXISTENTIAL READING

The term *existentialism* was defined by French philosopher Jean Paul Sartre as a humanistic philosophy in which "existence precedes essence" and in which "man is nothing else but that which he makes of himself" (Kaufmann [1956] 1975, 349). In his indispensable anthology of existential texts, Walter Kaufmann claims that Sartre's famous definition is "careless," that there is no one philosophy that represents the concept of existentialism ([1956] 1975, 45). In the 1960s, due to the popularity of French writers Jean Paul Sartre and Albert Camus, there emerged a number of literary and philosophical works that became identified by that name. Existentialism, Kauffman insists, cannot not be defined; it describes a number of attitudes or themes shared by a wide range of intellectuals practicing in Russia, Germany, Spain, and France. Of the many mutual themes to be found in Kaufmann's collection of existential writings from Dostoevsky to Sartre, there are three in particular that affect our reading of *The Death of Jim Loney:* the image of the stranger, the calculated use of a negative protagonist or antihero, and the "central existentialist motif of confrontation with death" (Kaufmann [1956] 1975, 41).

Albert Camus's *The Stranger (L'Etrangere)* was published in French in 1942 and first translated into English in 1946. It is the story of Meursault, an ordinary young man who lives in Algiers and works as a bookkeeper. The novel opens in a nursing home at the wake of Meursault's mother, whose death he takes in a matter-of-fact way, as if he were a stranger to her. His life goes along smoothly, according to routine; he has a girlfriend, goes to work, goes swimming, always dines at the same restaurant. He has none of the attributes of the conventional hero. Then one day on the beach in the blazing sun he irrationally shoots an Arab who is following his friend, Raymond. Meursault is arrested and found guilty of the murder, mainly on the basis that he had shown no emotion during his mother's funeral. At the trial he has the feeling that he is "the odd man out, a kind of intruder" (Camus [1942] 1988, 84). In jail, as his execution approaches, Meursault confronts his own death, refusing to accept the illusion of hope offered him by the prison chaplain. In a rage he attacks the chaplain, then feels a deliverance from hope and an acceptance of his fate: "As if that blind rage had washed me clean, rid me of hope; for the first time, in that night alive with signs and stars, I opened myself to the gentle indifference of the world" (Camus [1942] 1988, 122).

We asked Welch if he was familiar with *The Stranger*, to which his answer was an emphatic, "Sure." Welch told us, "I really like *The Stranger*. There's a simplicity in that book that really intrigued me when I read it" ("Montana Interview"). Like Meursault, Jim Loney is an ordinary young man. He has a girlfriend. He likes to drink and talk and make love. Then one day he irrationally shoots his friend, Myron Pretty Weasel. At the end of the book Loney confronts his death as he watches the blood from his arm "spattering the stones" (179). His final vision is of the dark bird, alive, flying to a "distant place" (179).

Jim Loney is, like Meursault, a person distant or alienated from his culture, a "stranger," a word that appears several times in *The Death of Jim Loney*. The one sympathetic tribal cop thinks that they have been "hunting a total stranger, a faceless stranger" (178). When Loney visits his father, he doesn't come as a son but as a "stranger to a stranger" (146). One reviewer recognizes Jim as "a stranger to contemporary society, his own heritage, and himself" (Klein 1979, 1722).

Camus had envisioned his nonhero or antihero as a stranger who was sure of nothing but himself, "sure of my life and sure of the death I had waiting for me" (120). Loney's certainty in his fallen world comes from booze, which eases his pain and makes him warm as he plans and awaits his execution (174–76). The fainthearted protagonist of each novel encounters an emptiness that makes death the only reasonable choice in an absurd or irrational universe. According to Welch, Loney "chose to accept death as a deliberate thing because he wanted to do something with his life. It would get him out of his routine of sitting around and drinking wine" ("Baltimore Interview"). While Welch's defense of Loney's death seems harsh, it makes absolute sense within the framework of the existential model of choice proposed in Camus's *The Stranger*.

*The Death of Jim Loney* resonates with certain existential themes found in mid-twentieth-century American fiction. Even without assuming a direct influence, one can speculate that Camus's classic French novel *The*

*Stranger* had an effect on James Welch, on Richard Wright, and on other American writers culturally divorced from mainstream values. This alienation is particularly evident in Richard Wright's *Native Son* (1940) and in Wright's short story, "The Man Who Lived Underground," published in *Cross Section* in 1944, a story that has been called "existentially philosophical" (Gibson 1997, 794). Each of these works is concerned with the concept of the stranger; the intentional use of a nonheroic protagonist or antihero; and the existential encounter with death. Jim Loney (lonely) lives in a ghetto not of his making, a quasi-prison that dates back to his ancestors' enslavement as Indians, whereas Bigger Thomas of *Native Son* and freddaniels, the nearly nameless anti-hero of "The Man Who Lived Underground," are freed, northern Blacks still enslaved by a plantation mentality. Welch was very much moved by *Native Son* when he read it: "I remember Bigger Thomas and that book as being extremely powerful. When you read things—and I read *Native Son* way back in college—I think they have a tendency to be there in the recesses of your mind, so that when you're stretching your imagination you let things come out. The story might be there. It's very powerful so I think it might have stuck with me" ("Baltimore Interview").

All three antiheroes are "Natives": one is Native American; two are Native Sons. All three men, accused of committing a murder and pursued by the police, run from the law without getting very far. Born as strangers and branded as criminals, they are put to death by a society that has no place for them. When the police officer in "The Man Who Lived Underground" says, "You've got to shoot his kind. They'd wreck things" (Wright [1942] 1968, 160), he could just as easily be describing Jim Loney.

As Bigger Thomas and freddaniels had sought their hiding place in the streets of Chicago, so Jim Loney seeks his in Mission Valley, in the Little Rockies. At the end of each work the protagonist, condemned to die, must confront his own death, just as Meursault confronted his from the prison in Algiers. Hated by the police, amputated from society, utterly alone, Jim Loney and freddaniels plunge to their deaths. The last sentence of *The Death of Jim Loney* begins: "And he fell, and as he was falling he felt a harsh wind where there was none" (179); the sentence concludes with the reference to the distant wings of a "dark bird" (179). The last sentence of "The Man Who Lived Underground" reads: "He sighed and closed his eyes, a whirling object rushing alone in the darkness, veering, tossing, lost in the heart of the earth" (Wright [1942] 1968, 160). With each death comes the fleeting knowledge that the antihero has opened himself to the nothingness of an absurd universe.

Although the overwhelming sense of alienation in *The Death of Jim Loney* suggests that the novel is an existential text, some critics stress the Indian themes instead. Kathleen Sands claims that the desolate hero has died to reaffirm his Native American heritage, symbolized by the dark bird. Loney's death thus fulfills the Gros Ventre vision quest and the return of the hero (Sands 1986, 131–32). Robert M. Nelson, who acknowledges Welch's possible debt to *The Stranger,* argues that the tone of despair in *The Death of Jim Loney* is not so much the by-product of a European influence as it is the direct expression of Native peoples. Nelson makes a convincing case when he groups Loney not with the existential antihero but with the dislocated Indian, citing Leslie Silko's *Ceremony* and N. Scott Momaday's *House Made of Dawn* to support his argument (Nelson 1993, 120–21).

Although an Indian-centered reading is surely an option, the resounding existential themes are inescapable. Like the muskrat in the trap, like the stranger on the beach, like Bigger in his cell and freddaniels in the sewer, Jim Loney falls to his death because he cannot control his fate in an irrational world. A modern Everyman caught in the snares of a dying culture, he has no choice but to will his own death.

# 5

# *Fools Crow*
# (1986)

## CHARACTER DEVELOPMENT

*Fools Crow,* if one defines the story by Western time and place, is a narrative about several Indian tribes who once lived in the subhills of the Rocky Mountains of Montana in 1870, the same year that American history books record as when Confederate General Robert E. Lee died. If, however, one describes the story in Blackfeet terms, it is a tale of life and death still being recollected in the memories of Indians living along the Backbone of the World below the Medicine Line separating the Siksikas and the Lone Eaters. Immediately upon entering the novel, the reader is thrust into an unfamiliar place populated by unfamiliar tribes (the Siksikas, the Entrails People) and strangely named characters (Eagle Ribs, Kills-close-to-the-lake) who elude one's memory in the early stages of the narrative. It therefore is useful to provide a guideline that first identifies the major characters and later locates their actions in the plot.

### The Nations

Welch identifies the three major tribes of the Blackfeet nation indirectly on the first page. The central and first-named character, White Man's Dog, contemplates the people who live to the north, south, and west of Chief Mountain, the strongest peak on the Backbone of the World: the Pikuni,

The Kainahs, and the Siksikas. These groups are further divided into societies or clans such as the Lone Eaters (the southern Blackfeet) and the Flat Head people (the Salish). Among the many other societies mentioned in *Fools Crow* are the All Crazy Dogs, the Raven Carriers, and the Tails (252). According to Walter McClintock, "men did not join the Blackfeet societies for pleasure but to fulfill vows, generally made because of sickness, or for some remarkable escape from danger. The leading societies ruled the camp, and helped the chiefs to administer public discipline (McClintock [1968] 1999, 464). In *Fools Crow* numerous societies interact or oppose each other, representing a diverse culture made up of distinct social groups, most of them unfamiliar to the modern reader.

White Man's Dog is a Blackfeet and a member of the Lone Eater's society, so named because a formed chief had the habit of avoiding breakfast guests by getting up early and eating alone (McClintock [1968] 1999, 201). In the first two pages of the text, White Man's Dog refers to his enemies from rival clans: the Parted Hairs (the Sioux) and the Entrails People (the Gros Ventre, who were the tribal ancestors of Welch's mother). These and other native peoples are identified in an indispensable map of Montana Territory printed at the very end of *Fools Crow*.

Far to the north lies the land of the whiskey traders. White Man's Dog envies their "many-shots guns which could bring down five blackhorns with five shots, which could kill an enemy from far off" (4). The guns are repeater rifles; the blackhorns are buffalo. White Man's Dog envies the traders, for with such a gun he could "bring about his own luck" (4). The enormous irony of *Fools Crow* is felt in these first pages, since the white trader or settler, the one whose weapons are desired, will in the future be the Indians' greatest enemy. The interveners are called by many names: traders, soldiers, "seizers" (253), settlers, "blue coated warriors" (93). All of these groups constitute the enemy and are known as the *Napikwans*, what the Sioux called the *Wasichus*, a term that meant "white man" but that did not always refer to skin color (Neihardt [1932] 1998, 8).

## Characters and Animals

For almost half of the novel the central character, whose birth name was Sinopa, is named White Man's Dog. He was given this name in jest because as a child he was constantly seen with an old storyteller, Victory Robe White Man (218). After he has distinguished himself as a warrior, he earns the name Fools Crow because he had fooled the Crow clan into losing their horses during a Pikuni raid. Within the unstated grammar of the name the reader assumes other words: "[He] fools [the] crow." Flatly pronounced, the title assumes the stereotypical speech pattern of the Indian as it is rendered in Hollywood films, with the subject of the clause deleted. Many of the names listed in the text have this grammatical incongruity: Talks Different (36); Heard-by-both-sides Woman (111); Kills-close-to-the-lake (125); Under Bull (209). As in *The Heartsong of Charging Elk*, so Welch's title *Fools Crow* not only contains the name of an animal but names the hero as well. Recall that in contrast, the central character of *Winter in the Blood* is nameless, having never earned a name.

Other major male characters are as follows: Rides-at-the-door, Fools Crow's father, who had "many horses and three wives" (3); Running Fisher, Fools Crow's handsome brother; Yellow Kidney, who leads the band on the Crow raid and is captured; Boss Ribs, father of Fast Horse, a young warrior whose loud boasting and disobedience result in Yellow Kidney's capture; Owl Child, an Indian who seeks bloody revenge against the *Napikwans* ; Heavy Runner, Mountain Chief, and Three Bears, three chiefs who attempt to negotiate with the "seizers"; and Mik'api, the medicine man who befriends Fools Crow and helps to initiate his quest.

The principal female characters are Double Strike Woman, Rides-at-the-door's first wife and Fools Crow's mother; Striped Face, Rides-at-the-door's second wife; Kills-close-to-the-lake, Rides-at-the-door's third and youngest wife, who is sent back to her father after having an affair with Running Fisher; Heavy Shield Woman, wife of Yellow Kidney and leader of the Sun Dance ceremony; and Red Paint, daughter of Heavy Shield Woman, who is Fools Crow's only wife and the mother of his child. The reader comes into contact with these and many more women, men, and children as they play out their daily lives in a cycle of 12 moons. They cure meat, they laugh, they make love in the same way that they had done for generation after generation.

With the coming of the horse and the consistent appearance of the buffalo herds, the Blackfeet and other Plains tribes had been able to develop a stable system of labor in which both genders played an interactive role. Barbara Cook argues that with the help of the horse, men were able to kill the buffalo in minutes, whereas it took women a far longer time to tan them. Because untreated buffalo skins were of no value in trading, women were essential workers in the gender-designated and polygamous society. Welch's "fully rounded" presentation of women helps to break down the stereotypical view that Indian women were treated like slaves (Cook 2000, 443).

In *Killing Custer* Welch credits the arrival of the horse in around 1730 with improving the lives of the Blackfeet (1994, 136). He remarks that the skins for tipis and lodges grew almost five times in number because the horses could carry them on the travois (139). Superior to dogs in size and strength, horses were an asset because they ate grass, not meat. What is more, horses rarely fought each other. They were valued by the entire community and marked the accumulation of wealth among the Plains people. Stealing horses became a war but also a game, an intertribal contest of victory and loss. "To steal horses was not only a means to obtain wealth but a chance to display courage and cunning, virtues which impressed potential young wives" (*Killing Custer* 1994, 138).

## Supernatural Characters

In addition to the Blackfeet people and their domesticated animals, there is a strong supernatural presence in the book, based on tales told to Welch by his elders and on his extensive reading of Blackfeet narratives. One of these figures is Na'pi or Old Man, the creator and trickster to whom White Man's Dog prays for guidance (*Fools Crow*, 55). But the most important figure from Blackfeet mythology is Scarface, also called Star Boy or Poia (*Fools Crow*, 349–352). He is the legendary hero on whom Fools Crow is to some extent modeled and whose significance is emphasized when Welch's hero says, "Of all the Above Ones he is most like us" (262).

Drawing on the writings of Walter McClintock, George Bird Grinnell, and other ethnographers, Nora Barry connects the journey of the cultural hero Scarface, son of Feather Woman and Morning Star, to the journey of Fools Crow. Both heroes go on a vision quest, and both are rewarded with visions. Scarface brings the Sun Dance ceremony back to the people, whereas Fools Crow gets to see the future by reading a skin presented to him by Feather Woman. Barry rightly insists, however, that though there are parallels, the stories are not identical. Fools Crow is a human and therefore incapable of reaching the Above Ones.

Cold Maker is a supernatural agent who figures prominently in the early raid on the Crow tribe. He lives in the Always Winter Land. In a dream he orders Fast Horse to remove a rock that had fallen across an ice spring on the side of Woman Don't Walk Butte. In his haste to reach the Crow camp, Fast Horse ignores the dream. Although Yellow Kidney is suspicious of Fast Horse's action, he too decides to go ahead without obeying Cold Maker's request. The fingers later missing from Yellow Kidney's hands result from Crow retaliation but also symbolically suggest the possibility of frostbite.

Feather Woman is the fallen wife of the Morning Star, forced to leave the Above Ones when she digs a forbidden turnip, much as her Judeo-Christian counterpart Eve is forced from Eden when she eats the forbidden fruit. Fools Crow has great sympathy for Feather Woman: "Her only sin was one of loneliness, then and now and forever" (360). Through her agency the future of his people is revealed to Fools Crow.

Within this hierarchy one discovers a number of marvelous animals, animals that not only intervene in human affairs but have the power to talk, tell jokes, suffer pain, and guide the hero on his quest. Fools Crow is guided by numerous animals—his horse, a raven, a wolverine, and a puppy. The strongest of these is Raven, who is intimate with Mik-api and serves as his messenger; according to Nora Barry, a talking bird was not uncommon in Blackfeet mythology (1991–92, 19, 12n). The other major animal is Skunk Bear or Wolverine, a ferocious variety of wolf that is Fools Crow's helper or tutelary spirit. The hero rescues Skunk Bear twice, once in wake-time and once in a vision. "All men were expected to seek a 'tutelary spirit' through a vision" (Brown 1997, 54). The animal presence in *Fools Crow* is an aspect of what some critics have called magical realism, a term examined here in the "Style" section. For Welch, talking animals were simply part of the belief system of the Blackfeet people. They were necessary to convey "the notion of another reality" (*American Audio Prose Library* 1985).

## The Naming of Characters

White Man's Dog earned his honored name, Fools Crow, through acts of courage. Naming was part of oral tradition among Plains Indians before the Napikwans arrived to rename the people, the rivers, the mountains. Joseph Epes Brown writes that among the Sioux, personal names "imply relationship, protection, favor, and influence from the source of the named. Names indicate affiliation, connote power, and have sacred import" (Brown 1997, 67). During the course of a lifetime, a male would have a birth name, perhaps the name of a grandparent. As a child he would have an informal play name and, as a man, a formal name earned through an act of valor or received in a vision. The Oglala Sioux roster of 1883 lists 373 names, almost two-thirds of which mention birds or animals (e.g., Black Elk, High-Wolf, No-Dog) (Brown 1997, 66–70).

The two animals most directly associated with Fools Crow are his earned-name animal, the crow, and his animal helper, the wolverine. In a two-volume set of medicine cards and explanatory text, Jamie Sams and

David Carson have compiled a pictorial guide to discovering the power of animals in American Indian life. The wolf, the raven, and the crow can be related to the plot and characterization of Welch's magical novel. Like Fools Crow, the wolf shows both loyalty to family as well as a "strongly individualistic urge" (Sams and Carson 1988, 97). The wolf is a teacher. The crow, the "keeper of all sacred law" (Sams and Carson 1988, 133), is capable of shifting shape and of recognizing that much of what appears to be reality is an illusion. Perhaps the qualities of the crow help to explain the power of prophecy granted to Fools Crow in his final vision. The raven, Mik-api's link between the natural and the spiritual realms, is associated with ceremonial magic, healing, and energy. "In any healing circle, Raven is present. Raven guides the magic of healing and the change in consciousness that will bring about a new reality and dispel the 'dis-ease' or illness" (Sams and Carson 1988, 102). At the end of *Fools Crow*, Mik-api leads a procession and the Pikuni pray that "after the sad winter they had lived through, there would be hope and joy this spring" (390). The old prophet's energy and cultural healing are attributable to his affinities with the messenger–Raven.

Joseph Epes Brown provides a chart at the end of his study that lists animals sacred to the Sioux. The wolf or wolverine has the male attributes of strength, courage, invisibility, swiftness, observation, and attentiveness. The crow, like the wolverine, has the masculine powers of swiftness, observation, and attentiveness (1997, 109–10). Applying these Sioux concepts to *Fools Crow*, it seems likely that Welch's protagonist is named to describe both his action and his character. He fools the Crow. He is strong, swift, observant, and attentive. Early in the novel Yellow Kidney compares him to a wolverine, "low and powerful" (20).

Walter McClintock, in *The Old North Trail*, one of Welch's acknowledged sources, outlines the Blackfeet naming process in a manner similar to Brown's depiction of the Oglala Sioux, although he adds that "the names of females were not changed after childhood as was the case with males" (McClintock [1968] 1999, 399). McClintock's direct contact with Blackfeet naming practices is an invaluable help in understanding Welch's choices and a fascinating document in its own right. He emphasizes the prominence of horses in many Blackfeet names: "The use of horses and the capture of horses from other tribes having been a prominent feature of their life, it was but natural that the word horse was used in a great variety of name combinations" (McClintock [1968] 1999, 397). Welch's horse names—Fast Horse, Many Horses, and Spotted Horse People—are consistent with this pattern. Less obvious is a name like "Ah-kit-kats-a-pinsoye," which means "his eyes are dry because he is always looking or staring" (McClintock [1968]; 1999, 402). A few of Welch's names are similarly elusive—for example, Everybody-talks-about-him (110) and Head Carrier (68).

During a visit to a large Blackfeet camp McClintock talks with Brings-down-the-Sun, a chief who understands the language of birds and knows what they are saying to each other. The chief translates the messages of woodpeckers to bugs, of the king bird to berries. He notes the special wisdom of the raven, who tells the tribe where they might find meat or where they might expect an ambush (McClintock [1968] 1999, 481–84). It takes only one more leap of the imagination before we have the laughing, joking Raven who talks to Mik-api in *Fools Crow.*

The raven is "a large bird of the crow family." Its second meaning is "to devour greedily" (*Webster's New International Dictionary of the English Language,* 1949). Looking at Fools Crow with these attributes in mind, he is the character who finds meat for the impoverished Heavy Shield Woman during Yellow Kidney's absence. He foresees the Crow's ambush during the raid on the Crow camp. But he "fools [the] Crow," a tribe that had long been the enemy of the Blackfeet and a tribe known for its greed. Thus he earns his noble name.

Other studies of Indian literature and culture comment on naming practices. Laura Stookey, writing about the novels of Louise Erdrich, lists naming as one of Erdrich's themes. Erdrich's ancestors were known by several different names: the Anishinabe, a name that predates European contact; the Ojibwa, the northern branch of the Anishinabe, the people whom the French named the Saulteur; and the Chippewa, Indians living in North Dakota (Stookey 1999, 9). Albertine, a character in *The Bingo Palace,* begins to research her ancestry shortly after her naming ceremony. Cally, in *The Antelope Wife,* also remembers her naming ceremony but does not know the meaning of her "spirit name" (Stookey 1999, 132). Stookey uses naming for the purposes of identity, theme, and characterization as she explores Erdrich's technique of plot development.

## PLOT DEVELOPMENT

*Fools Crow* is a novel meant to capture the lives of an entire people at a given stage of history. Although no single character can bear the weight of so enormous a project, White Man's Dog, later named Fools Crow, eventually earns the right to that distinction by virtue of both his heroism and his knowledge of his culture. If the plot, then, can be said to have a center, that center is the story of White Man's Dog.

Although the emotional source for Welch's tales about Blackfeet life and culture was his paternal grandmother, there were written sources as well: James Willard Schultz's *My Life as an Indian* ([1907] 1983), John Ewers's *The Blackfeet Raiders of the Plains* (1965), Henry Bird Grinnell's *Blackfoot Lodge Tales* ([1892] 1962), and Walter McClintock's *The Old North Trail* ([1968] 1999). He told William Bevis that although these books taught him certain important facts about Blackfeet life, none of them helped him to "dramatize within" ("Wylie Tales" 1995, 9). An accomplished novelist, Welch was able to convert these frequently dry sources into the matter of fiction.

Much of the early action in *Fools Crow* involves the competition between two rival tribes, the Lone Eaters, a Pikuni society, and their long-term enemies, the Crow. In vivid detail Welch describes the Lone Eaters' raid on the Crows: their walking by day to avoid being exposed by Night Red Light; their painting their bodies for strength; their praying to Sun Chief for a safe return. There is tremendous power in this early sequence, the kind of excitement that has been visualized in cinema and that Welch captures in prose. Much of the thrill is owed to the horses, the ones they ride and the ones they are stealing. As Welch explains in *Killing Custer*: "Perhaps more than anything, the horse brought new excitement into the lives of the Plains Indians. Suddenly they could move as fast as the wind, they could chase down enemies and game, which before the arrival of the horse would have been an empty wish" (1994, 139).

Although the raid is successful, there are two setbacks: White Man's Dog is forced to kill a young Crow boy to silence him, and Yellow Kidney, leader of the raid, has disappeared. When the horse hunters return, Kills-close-to-the-lake unsuccessfully tempts White Man's Dog to have sex with her. He refuses in reality but later submits in a dream. When she seduces his brother, Running Fisher, she is sent home to her father, and her lover is banished to the clan of his mother, Striped Woman.

Eventually White Man's Dog receives his new name, Fools Crow, at a ceremony in his honor. He has married his early love, Red Paint, and has achieved respectability. The couple go on a journey together, and Red Paint learns she has conceived. On the journey Raven orders Fools Crow to kill an offensive Napikwan, a thoughtless hunter who kills animals and leaves the meat to rot. Using his wife as bait, Fools Crow obeys Raven and slaughters the hairy Napikwan, who is suspected of lusting after Red Paint. Nora Barry sees the killing of the Napikwan as analogous to killing the monster in the Western epic tradition (Barry 1991–92, 10). Another critic uses the monster image, judging the passage to be stereotyped and arguing that it reveals "Welch's almost flat characterization of this monster" (Shanley 1996, 136).

After Fools Crow tells the tribal council of his encounter with the Napikwan, the elders decide that there will be no more killing of settlers. With the passage of the moons Fools Crow learns to accept the wisdom of the tribe and the medicine taught to him by Mik-api. The final sections of the novel follow Fools Crow on his vision quest under the guidance of Skunk Bear, or wolverine. After meeting Feather Woman in a dream/ vision, he gains the dreadful knowledge that his people will suffer disease and death. His reward is knowing that the traditions will survive.

## NARRATIVE POINT OF VIEW

*Fools Crow* opens in the third person as a young man of 18 winters watches black clouds circling the sky. Almost 30 pages later, White Man's Dog tells his father, Rides-at-the-door, about a raid and about the disappearance of Yellow Kidney, the leader of the raid. Almost simultaneously Yellow Kidney has been captured by the Crow and his fingers cut off to render him incapable of performing the major functions of a Blackfeet man—hunting, fighting, and protecting his women. The reader does not learn of Yellow Kidney's fate, however, until he returns to camp and recounts his story to the people smoking pipes at the lodge of Three Bears. Yellow Kidney tells his story, which runs for eight pages, in the first-person narrative voice. The story begins, "This then is my story" (72) and is interrupted by an occasional response or reaction: "But go on, Yellow Kidney, tell us how you survived your misfortune" (78). The story ends when Yellow Kidney runs out of the narrative energy to keep going. Then the narrative shifts, without transition, from Yellow Kidney's first-person account of his disastrous journey to a third-person description of Fast Horse leaving the camp in secrecy.

In a similar method of narration we hear Boss Ribs's story of the origin of Beaver Medicine (195–98). During a pipe-smoking ceremony, Fools Crow tells his tribe of his journey into the mountains and his encounter with the lustful Napikwan. The personal story is followed by a tribal council in which Rides-at-the-door speaks, the militant Young Bird Chief responds, and Rides-at-the-door speaks again. Thus Fools Crow's story generates a debate that ends with Three Bears's instruction: "Let there be no more killing of the Napikwans. Let the Lone Eaters be known as men of wisdom who put the good of their people before their individual honor" (178).

The constant shifts from first to third person do more than enable Welch to create an atmosphere. They also serve to draw the "we" or "us" into the communal debate. The first-person "we" in this episode represents a double construction, one that includes not only the fictional characters present at the lodge but also the informed reader, who becomes a privileged participant at the storytelling ceremonies, an eavesdropper in this oral-to-written experiment in fiction.

Overriding the numerous first-person stories is a third-person omniscient narrator whose authority controls the written text. The narrator is assumed to be James Welch. Reconstructing the history through careful research and a literary imagination, Welch becomes the mediator between past and present. By setting his novel in the historical past, he has recreated a world that "Native writers have assiduously avoided" (King 1987, 1223). A contemporary Indian novelist, he is also an immortal Blackfeet, heir to a tradition that once measured time by the position of the moon and the falling of leaves.

## STRUCTURE

### The Quest

Chapter 2 provides a discussion of the vision quest in the Blackfeet oral tradition. In his novels Welch uses this motif in both a suggestive and a deliberate way. Whereas in *Winter in the Blood* and *The Death of Jim Loney* the vision quest is a cultural element that remains in the background, in *Fools Crow* it is all-encompassing, because it determines the development of the plot from beginning through middle until the end, moving, in circular fashion, from end back to the beginning, back to a time of plentitude for the Blackfeet.

White Man's Dog leaves the community not once but several times, in each instance gaining a greater reputation in his quest for fulfillment. At the beginning of *Fools Crow* the hero is an immature young man who has yet to participate in a horse raid. Throughout the course of the novel one can trace the changes in his character as he moves toward heroism. Isolated from the community, he performs the ritual functions of fasting and spirituality. He seeks his tutelary spirit, gains wisdom, and becomes the new prophet. The structure of the novel, in other words, is almost completely parallel to the hero's development as a character. The end replicates the beginning, relying on a circularity that involves, like much of Welch's fiction, "a community-based ritual of immersion into isolation followed by a resurfacing into community" (Norden 1994, 78).

## The Return

*Fools Crow* is "about returning, about going home to an identity, about looking back through the hole in time" (Owens 1992, 165). In *Fools Crow* there is a complex series of returns. The first of these involves the Pikuni's return from their raid on the Crow tribe. The community greets the returning braves with shouts of triumph. But one prestigious member of the clan, Yellow Kidney, does not return with the raiding party. Left behind because of Fast Horse's noisy boasting, he hides in a lodge, where he is guilty of fornicating with a Crow girl who is dying of smallpox. Because he has robbed her of a virtuous death, the dishonored leader realizes that he has "taken the path traveled only by the meanest of scavengers" (81). The Crows discover him and cut off his fingers; the Spotted Horse People (the Cheyenne), who find him on the brink of death, nurse him back to health. Fast Horse, the warrior initially responsible for Yellow Kidney's bad luck, is the one who returns him to the people. Defeated and despairing, Yellow Kidney nonetheless experiences a gradual healing process after he is reunited with the Lone Eaters and with his family. Ironically, Yellow Kidney later leaves the community and is murdered by a Napikwan whose only motive is to kill an Indian.

In the meantime, Fast Horse had "become an outsider within his own band" (70). While Fools Crow's success as a horse raider has won him respect, Fast Horse's failure as dream interpreter brings him shame. He is Welch's example of an outsider, a person lacking relatedness. "You're an outsider, you're leaving the tribe. Then you have nobody. As long as you are part of the tribe, as long as you are related, you're in good shape" ("Montana Interview"). Unable to sense relationship, Fast Horse leaves the Lone Eaters and joins forces with Owl Child, who is Welch's version of the savage, murdering, scalp-hunting Indian. Another failed warrior is Fools Crow's brother, banished from the tribe for having sex with Rides-at-the-doors's third wife. These permanent departures are meant to contrast with the several returns of Fools Crow, whose actions unify him with the community and are an aspect of the *mitakuye oyasin* ("all are related") philosophy discussed in earlier chapters.

Although these secondary departures and returns add complexity to the novel, it is Fools Crow's movements that structure the plot. He leaves the community on a number of journeys: one to earn his manhood; another to get vengeance against the Crow villain who mutilated Yellow Kidney; another to visit the Backbone of the World with his wife, Red Paint; and the last to fulfill his mission as prophet.

Perhaps the most ambivalent return in the novel occurs in Mik-api's final prophecy. He foresees the blackhorn, or buffalo, returning to the plains once more, as if they had never vanished, as it was in the beginning: "The blackhorns had returned and, all around, it was as it should be" (391). Why does the joyous fulfillment of this final vision run counter to Fools Crow's tragic reading of the magic skin? Does myth transcend reality? Is there a Second Coming? Or is the circle forever broken, a question that Black Elk asks after he witnessed the butchering of the Sioux at Wounded Knee: "And I, to whom so great a vision was given in my youth,—you see me now a pitiful old man who has done nothing, for the nation's hoop is broken and scattered. There is no center any longer, and the sacred tree is dead" (Neihardt [1932] 1998, 270). Although there are no definitive answers to these questions, there is an attempt, at least, to explore them more fully in the final section of this chapter.

## GENRE

Like *Black Elk Speaks, Fools Crow* dramatically conveys the plight of Native Americans in the nineteenth century. Robert L. Berner claims that in its comprehensive treatment of the spiritual life of a culture, *Black Elk Speaks* is "the only work that can bear comparison" to *Fools Crow* (1987, 333). Both works contain elements of the *bildungsroman*, a literary work that traces "the development of a young person, usually from adolescence to maturity" (Harmon and Holman 2000, 59). The prophet Black Elk begins his story with his birth in the Moon of the Popping Trees in 1863 (Neihardt [1932] 1998, 7). He remembers that when he was five he began to hear voices: "It was like somebody calling me, and I thought it was my mother, but there was nobody there" (18). As a nine-year-old Black Elk experiences his great vision of the Six Grandfathers and the flaming rainbow, cited in Chapter 2. At the end of the autobiography, his great vision now a dim memory, Black Elk laments the failure of his dream and the collapse of the sacred center.

The prophet Fools Crow begins his apprenticeship as White Man's Dog, with "little to show for his eighteen winters" (3). At the end of the novel he envisions a broken nation and a people afflicted by disease and the loss of hope. But whereas *Black Elk Speaks* is an oral history recorded in writing by John G. Neihardt, *Fools Crow* is an historical novel set in Montana Territory in 1870 and filtered through the imagination of its creator, James Welch. As author, Welch is the only one who can mediate between the spirit world and history. Although Welch may have been thinking about the historic Black Elk, Fools Crow is of his own invention, a character who bridges the gap between history and myth. As Hans Bak so eloquently writes, "The novel stands as both a personal and a communal act of recovery and remembrance, a symbolic restoration of voice to the voiceless, history to the uprooted, legacy to the lost" (Bak 1995, 36).

Hans Bak, Ron McFarland, and other critics claim that the strength of *Fools Crow* derives from its combination of epic structure with Blackfeet legend. An epic by European standards is a long poem that tells a story, in elevated style, about a hero who is a representative of his or her people and their history. The hero conducts a journey in which he or she "engages with supernatural forces and performs deeds of great valor" (Harmon and Holman 2000, 188–89). Both as prophet and warrior, Fools Crow meets the qualifications of an epic hero. Ron McFarland notes that like the classical epic, Fools Crow begins *in medias res* (in the beginning of things) and has a central hero who, in his piety and his concern for community, resembles Virgil's Aeneas. McFarland further notes the descent into the Underworld that was part of Aeneas's prophecy and that finds its parallel in Welch's Feather Woman episode (2000, 114–15; 122–25).

In addition to the comparisons with *The Aeneid*, though, McFarland clearly places Welch's hero within the enormous body of Blackfeet legends collected by scholars. In Fools Crow's final vision, history and myth coalesce. "Welch moves his hero from the personal, secular level to the tribal, mythic level of his epic development" (Barry 1991–92, 13).

## STYLE

### Translation

Welch's epic storytelling is almost completely bound to his style or manner of telling. As such, style can barely be separated from the language that generates it. Languages differed considerably among the Plains Indians, even within the same linguistic family; for example, the Cree and Blackfeet were both Algonquian speakers but they "could not understand each other" (Taylor 1997, 13). As a contemporary Native American writer Welch is faced with the difficult task of reflecting the Algonquian spoken language (which he, ironically, does not speak) while making his never-told story coherent to modern readers, the majority of whom are literate European and American editors, publishers, students, and scholars. For a Native American writer like Welch, the task is difficult, for he is re-creating the Blackfeet, a people as remote from the European imagination before Lewis and Clark's arrival in 1806 as Ed Sullivan would have been before the advent of television. In researching the lives of his Pikuni ancestors, Welch needed to elicit a language equal to the theme, in a style that would reflect their reality and would "edify other people who have been insisting on defining and naming tribal peoples for centuries" (Teuton 2001, 627).

To convey the ordinary lives of a small Blackfeet nation before the settlers arrived would mean renaming the already renamed mountains, the rivers, and the calendar. It meant that Welch had to invent a style that approached the literary art of translating by inventing what is called a *calque,* or literal translation from one language to another (McFarland 2000, 111). Translation from the spoken to the written language is a technique that in the European tradition dates back to Homer's rendering of the ancient Greek oral legends into *The Iliad* and *The Odyssey* in the ninth century B.C. Working within a similar framework, Welch translates the language and rituals of his nineteenth-century ancestors into a twentieth-century written text. To do so he must perform an act of literary reappropriation, which is, as Hans Bak states, "foremost a matter of language, of re-naming the specifics of place, person, and environment, historical event" (Bak 1995, 46). Fools Crow's allies are the Hard Topknots, the Small Robes, the Small Brittle Fats (175). The afterlife is called the Sand Hills or Shadowland (175). White Grass Woman is married to Skunk Cap (223). Modern readers may be bewildered by Welch's renaming of characters and places, perhaps forgetting that many European names at one time had a meaning associated with a trade or a characteristic (e.g., Miller, Carpenter, Fletcher, Grand, Gates, Smith).

In converting the orally grounded narrative of *Fools Crow* into a piece of writing, Welch uses many of the stylistic techniques that are observable in Chinua Achebe's *Things Fall Apart* ([1968] 1995) and Maxine Hong Kingston's *The Woman Warrior* ([1975] 1989). Each of these writers responded to a comparable dilemma: how to make the language and customs of the ancestors intelligible to a postcolonial readership. The tribe Achebe brings back to life are the Ibo of West Africa, whose gods and language were almost destroyed by the British in the mid-nineteenth century under the reign of Queen Victoria. Kingston traces her ancestry to Ts'ai Yen, a poet from the second century A.D. The tribe Welch resurrects are the Blackfeet of Montana, whose rituals and legends were nearly obliterated by westward-bound settlers in the cooling-off period following the Civil War.

To surmount the obstacles between past and present Achebe, Welch, and Kingston employ a strategy that might be called parenthetical translation: first naming an unfamiliar object and then describing it through indirect reference. Welch, for example, refers to smallpox as "white-scabs disease" and describes a mirror as "the-ice-that-looks-back" (16). These words are used in a context so that the meanings are soon clear. Readers unfamiliar with characters, terms, and events are best served by a glossary that would make the text more user-friendly. Achebe's publisher provides a convenient list of terms and characters at the end of the novel. Welch's and Kingston's do not.

## Magical Realism

For Welch to be authentic, his singing wolverine could not appear to be obtrusive or ridiculous. In *The Woman Warrior* Maxine Hong Kingston faced a similar stylistic issue: How does one present an authentic portrayal of a reality populated by ghosts? The narrator's mother has the custom of calling her ghosts by names that sound like Welch's. She was "good at naming—Wall Ghost, Frog Spirit (frogs are 'heavenly chickens'), Eating Partner" (Kingston [1975] 1989, 65). The ghosts are physically present. One storyteller says that "ghosts come right into the room. Once our whole family saw wine cups spinning and incense sticks waving through the air" (65).

Many critics have called this kind of fiction "magical realism." Although the term was first used by German art critic Franz Roh, it has been conveniently applied to literature, in particular to the kind of literature that combines fantasy and reality without having to justify the strangeness of events or characters (Majher, 2001, 1–2). Bruce Holland Rogers claims that magical realism is a "serious" form of writing that tells stories from the point of view of "people who live in our world and experience a different reality from the one we call objective. If there is a ghost in a story of magical realism, the ghost is not a fantasy element but a manifestation of the reality of people who believe in and have a 'real' experience of ghosts" (Rogers 2003, 2). Rogers refers to Leslie Marmon Silko's *Ceremony* as a good example of magical realism. The *Woman Warrior* and *Things Fall Apart*, with its talking oracle, are other good examples. All of them share with *Fools Crow* a supernatural quality in the sense that they are "super" or outside natural forces. Like the Chinese shaman of *The Woman Warrior*,

Welch's Mik-api is the mediator between the supernatural and the real, between the Raven and Fools Crow, who is the Raven's servant.

Magical realism is at its most useful when used to "explore the realities of characters or communities who are outside of the objective mainstream of our culture," such as "South Americans, Indians, or African slaves" (Rogers 2003, 4)—really, of anyone whose belief systems are unfamiliar to the average American. Some students of literature tend to disbelieve in the reality of the oracle of Delphi who warns Oedipus he will kill his father and marry his mother. They brand as superstition the oracle of the Ibo of Nigeria, Ifa, goddess of fertility in *Things Fall Apart*. Welch's reconceptualization of the past is no stranger a projection than these. It is a time when ravens spoke and wolverines chanted their power song.

When William Bevis questioned Welch's reluctance to distinguish between myth and reality, Welch responded in his matter-of-fact way. He said that he was pleased with the way Fools Crow's vision of the wolverine's biting Kills-close-to-the-lake just happened to work out: "I was kind of on a roll when I wrote that particular piece . . . so I let it go to a conclusion" ("Wylie Tales" 1995, 10). One senses very little theoretical sophistication behind Welch's response. If he is using the techniques of magical realism, he does so in some uncontrollable way, allowing the Pikuni "their sense of reality" ("Wylie Tales" 1995, 10). Or, as Peter Wild insists, the reality and the dream intermingle "until neither we nor the characters themselves can tell the difference. This is the book's major accomplishment" (1986, 14).

## SETTING AND THEME

Once upon a time there was a vast and unmapped territory inhabited by the Lone Eaters and the Entrails People and the Spotted Horse People. They lived in a climate so chilling that during the winter moon one could see mile after mile of ice, toward the glacier dwelling of Cold Maker and his daughters. As the Greeks had Apollo's chariot, so the Blackfeet had their Sun Chief: "The thin clouds that had been following them from the north had disappeared and Sun Chief rode high in the early afternoon sky" (18). At times Welch describes the natural world in terms of the supernatural. Or he will make use of color or sound to evoke setting: The sky was so blue that "the mountains looked like blue metal in the bright light" (53); "The only sound was the steady murmur of the river itself" (300).

The landscape of *Fools Crow* is limitless, sacred, breathing. It has "[no] freeways, fences, none of the symbols of modern alienation Welch has used so effectively in his previous work. Trading posts and forts, and a few ranches intrude upon the land, representing the growing conflict between tribes and whitemen, but they do not dominate" (Sands 1987, 81). The setting is vast, of epic proportions—a landscape that signifies "great nations, the world, or the universe" (Harmon and Holman 2000, 189).

Yet the setting is also intensely human, human in a period of time that predates modern technology. In the discussion of ecological criticism in *Winter in the Blood,* I note the intensity of the natural world and of natural functions. Although there is similar emphasis on these functions in *Fools Crow,* their effect on the reader is less obvious because personal privacy is less a part of the consciousness of his characters. Ironically, one of the most lyrical passages in the book is framed within an early-morning urination in which there is no shame, no secrecy, only White Man's Dog's elation at the smell of the grass, the song of the yellow-breast, the lightening of the morning sky (115).

The first sentence of the novel is an example of how Welch generally conveys setting. "Now that the weather had changed, the moon of the falling leaves turned white in the blackening sky and White Man's Dog was restless." Rather than naming the month, the settlers' way of measuring time, the narrator names the moon phase. Colors of black and white are used for contrast. The words *changed* and *restless* are part of the physical and emotional description, but they also point to one of the novel's major themes—the change in culture wrought by the Napikwans.

Throughout the novel a variety of legends, stories, ceremonies, and rituals contribute to the setting. The most sacred ceremony of the Plains Indians is the summer celebration of the Sun Dance. Welch devotes a considerable number of pages to this ceremony, which is a testing ground for the hero and his tribe but also for Heavy Shield Woman, who has vowed to lead the Sun Dance if Yellow Kidney is safely returned to the camp. At the approach of the "moon of flowers," the Pikuni people begin the annual journey to the Milk River to celebrate the Sun Dance, an event that Welch describes in terms that involve changes—in the moon, the sun, the grass, the camp location, and the geography.

What does not change is the ceremony itself. Heavy Shield Woman holds the medicine pouch of her predecessor as she begins her four-day fast, it being a Blackfeet custom to transfer the medicine bundle from one person to another (Versluis 1999, 63). Bands of people from different societies perform traditional dances in honor of Sun Chief. The men, led by Mik-api, conduct rites of purification, while a few of the bravest, including

Fools Crow, attach skewers to each breast and circle the Medicine Pole. Fools Crow "felt the sticky warm blood coursing down from his wounds" (116). After the flesh pulls free he falls "backward into the darkness" (117). That night, as if inspired by the intensity of the torture, he enters his dream of saving the wolverine from his trap. Arthur Versluis comments that the fasting, dancing, and self-torture of the Sun Dance often resulted in a visionary experience (Versluis 1999, 65).

There are several noticeable features about the Sun Dance sequence in *Fools Crow*. First is the sudden shift of setting from the real world of ceremony to the mythical realm of dream. Second is the coordination of elements of setting, such as the Medicine Pole and the sacred circle, within the fictional devices of plot and characterization. Third is the overwhelming sense of unity or oneness among the people assembled together for the Sun Dance, a unity created through images of the circle and through the repetition of ceremonial drum beats, which punctuate the entire section (114–16). Through graphic depictions of an environment as old as history, Welch is able to re-create the customs of his ancestors. The setting is not very different from what today is called Big Sky. As Kathleen Sands observes, Welch does not need to invent a setting in *Fools Crow*. It's already there, in an environment energized by the power of myth. "He is part of a continuum of connections between people, animals, stars, cycles of seasons and ceremonies stretching into the mythic past" (Sands 1987, 83).

*Mitakuye oyasin.* All are related.

## ALTERNATIVE READING: ARCHETYPAL CRITICISM

The word *archetype* goes back to the Greek words meaning *arche* (original) and *typos* (form). It is best recognized through the writings of Swiss psychoanalyst Carl Jung (Groden and Kreiswirth 1994, 36). According to Jung (1875–1961), archetypes are "forms or images of a collective nature which occur practically all over the earth as constituents of myths and at the same time as autochthonous [original or self-generating], individual products of unconscious origin" (Jung 1938, 63). For an individual, the unconscious or unknown matters of the mind would be revealed through dreams; for a culture, the unknown would be revealed collectively, through its mythology.

According to Maud Bodkin, one finds in literature a "form or pattern which persists amid variation from age to age, and which corresponds to a pattern or configuration of emotional tendencies in the minds of those who are stirred by the theme" (Bodkin [1934] 1961, 4). Although archetypal criticism is closely aligned with depth psychology, it is far more generalized than the Freudian branch of psychoanalytic criticism. It relies on broad cultural patterns (the Rebirth Archetype, the Universal Mother) rather than on more particularized, scientific constructs (the Oedipus Complex, the oral stage). Because of its diverse applicability, archetypal criticism has become a useful tool in the analysis of literature—for example, when it is applied to the significance of gender (Groden and Kreiswirth 1994, 39).

The archetypal critic reads literature for its references to myth and dream in order to gain a greater knowledge of the hero's or heroine's psyche as it relates to the aspirations of the nation he or she represents. Through an investigation of archetypes the critic can also come into closer contact with his or her own dreams and myths and gain a better understanding of the self.

This alternative reading examines a few of the major ideas of archetypal criticism as they relate to three specific patterns found in *Fools Crow:* the hero, the dream, and the gods. The primary source for the investigation is Joseph Campbell's *The Hero with a Thousand Faces,* published in 1956. In this text Campbell is concerned with the mythological foundations of all heroes, from the Minotaur or bull monster of ancient Greece to the Algonquin hero Manabozho (Campbell 1956, 90, 56n). Manabozho is one of several references to Indians in *The Hero with a Thousand Faces;* another is the Blackfeet hero Kut-o-yis or Blood Clot, who grew from clot to man in one day (Campbell 1956, 338–340; see Wissler and Duvall [1908] 1995 for a summary of the Blood Clot legend).

In his late-life television interviews with Bill Moyers, published in 1991 as *The Power of Myth,* Campbell is even more focused on American culture. Here his discourse includes the Blackfeet origin myth and buffalo mythology as well as more current topics such as drugs, football, film, and democracy. But though the application has changed, Campbell's ideas have remained essentially the same, and essentially positive, since the mid-1950s: "It has always been the prime function of mythology and rite to supply the symbols that carry the human spirit forward, in counteraction to those other human fantasies that tend to tie it back" (Campbell 1956, 11).

The hero of *Fools Crow* is an archetypal figure who follows the standard path of *separation-initiation-return* outlined by Campbell (Campbell 1956, 30, emphasis in original). Campbell aptly demonstrates this path in Judaism, Buddhism, and Hinduism; in Greek narrative; among the warriors of Bali; among the Pawnees of northern Kansas (Campbell 1956, 41). As emphasized throughout this book, the same pattern of separation-initiation-return dominates the structure of Blackfeet folk tales and of Welch's fiction. Fools Crow's return to the community at various junctures of the novel signals his affiliation with the culture. Like the Roman hero Aeneas, who rejects the temptation of Dido's love, Fools Crow sacrifices his personal dreams for the greater good of the people (McFarland 2000, 120).

We know the hero through his dreams, just as we know the Pikuni through their myths. Joseph Campbell, Otto Rank, and other psychoanalysts have made this crucial connection between dream symbolism and the hero myth (Rank 1957, 69). Welch uses dream symbolism effectively in all of his texts, often in terms of gender. We have reviewed the protagonist's nightmare of his mother giving birth to a duck in *Winter in the Blood*, and we have seen the mother's dream visitations to her son in *The Death of Jim Loney*. In *Fools Crow* dreams become a paramount source of information. They are a form of visionary experience, a means of communication, and a threshold to prophecy. Through them Fools Crow prepares for his vision quest. In them he rescues his totem animal, makes contact with Feather Woman, and receives the medicine bundle. Using these powers he is able to predict the fall of his people. In his final dream the hero experiences great pain but withholds the truth, as if he were the only hero among the Pikuni strong enough to endure the dream world, which is the gateway to the mythic realm of the gods. "Every night," explains one contemporary analyst, "we enter a mythic realm, a dark, primordial labyrinth, inhabited by the gods and ghosts of our ancestors, and glean from them some of the ancient wisdom of our kind" (Stevens 1995, 4).

The gods and ghosts of the ancestors often exact cruel payment from mortals. Fast Horse's exile, for example, is the inevitable result of his disregarding the wishes of Cold Maker. Sun Chief, father of Morning Star, sends his son's disobedient wife, Feather Woman, back to earth when she unintentionally disturbs the roots of the sacred turnip. She, in turn, passes on to Fools Crow the living skin whose shifting scenes are the cause of his agony. In her intervention Feather Woman marks the stage in the hero's initiation that Campbell calls "the Meeting with the Goddess"; he develops through a number of examples from world mythology, including Medusa, Parvati, and the Virgin Mary: "She is mother, sister, mistress, bride. Whatever in the world has lured, whatever has seemed to promise joy, has been premonitory [forewarned] of her existence—in the deep of sleep if not in the cities and forests of the world" (Campbell 1956, 111). Maud Bodkin devotes an entire section of *Archetypal Patterns in Poetry* to the mother or earth-goddess (Bodkin [1934] 1961, 148–210). Although the goddess is usually benign, she is also the "forbidding mother" (Campbell 1956, 111), a negative role that she seems to play in *Fools Crow.*

Of the Pikuni gods and goddesses, the most important is Sun Chief. He is the source of light and the venerated center of the Sun Dance ceremony, the major ritual for the people of the Plains. Campbell defines ritual as "the enactment of a myth. By participating in a ritual you are participating in a myth," much as a Jewish boy would participate in a bar mitzvah (Campbell 1991, 103). "Rituals are the form, the crystallization, of the mythological and religious cycles that not only make sense of the cosmos, but in fact reveal, augment, and even bring about human beings' harmony with it, and its harmony with them" (Versluis 1999, 49–50). To express gratitude for the granting of a favor or to atone for their misdeeds, many Indian men would perform the Sun Dance ritual, piercing their breasts with hooks and circling the Medicine Pole. Yet out of their suffering came renewal. "The overall importance of the Sun Dance was the renewal of personal spirituality as well as the renewal of the living earth, a time when kinships within both the social and natural realms were reaffirmed" ("Spirituality and the Sun Dance" 1998, 5).

Earlier we had pointed to the ambivalence of the novel's final vision. Mik-api, the keeper of the medicine, looks out on the plains and sees joy. He conducts a ceremony that heralds the Real-bear and elk; that displays the singing of songs from horses, owls, and buffalo; that celebrates the ceremonial wearing of elk skin robes; and that proclaims the reappearance of the vanished buffalo herds. He welcomes the return of the buffalo: "The blackhorns had returned and, all around, it was as it should be" (391). Nowhere else in the novel does the reader so strongly sense that myth is the collective dream of a people, the dream of a Second Return to a former order. Yet the dream contradicts the images on the yellow skin that Feather Woman had given Fools Crow in which he had seen "the end of the black-horns and the starvation of the Pikunis" (358).

Does mythology somehow account for both sides of the yellow skin: the good and the bad or, in Christian terms, the angel and the devil? Can any good come from the destruction of a people? Is the circle forever broken and all hope gone, as in Black Elk's lament after the Wounded Knee Massacre (Neihardt [1932] 1998, 270)? As in Chief Red Cloud's lament that "there was no hope on earth and God seemed to have forgotten us" (cited by Brown [1970] 1991, 439)?

In *The Power of Myth* Campbell describes the cultural transition that occurred when the horse came to the Plains Indians. "At this time, the

mythology transforms from a vegetation mythology to a buffalo mythology" (Campbell 1991, 106). And with the coming of the Napikwan, what
then? Is there then a transformation to a reservation mythology? Or a
prison mythology? Or is it a brighter future, perhaps, with the new
prophets—Russell Means, Chris Eyre, Joy Harjo, James Welch—being integrated into the timeless fabric of Indian dream making? As literary shaman, James Welch is the mediator between myth and dream, between the
people and their gods. Perhaps he can prepare us for the future by hand-
ing down the stories, even though, like Fools Crow, he is powerless to
change it.

# 6

# *The Indian Lawyer*
# (1991)

After completing *Fools Crow* in 1986, Welch began to shift his attention to the plight of the urban Indian, the person who leaves the reservation and its traditions in order to become assimilated in a city environment. In talking about how *The Indian Lawyer* relates to his earlier novels, Welch said that he tried to do something different in each:

> My first two novels, *Winter in the Blood* and *The Death of Jim Loney*, were about a couple of Indian men who had problems with identity. Then I wrote *Fools Crow* to sort of tell where these guys might have come from, given an historical context. Then with *The Indian Lawyer* what I wanted to do was to talk about a whole different kind of Indian who is very successful. He has been rising rapidly into this position where he's in a big law firm in Helena and he is running for congress. I wanted to write about a person who is successful by anybody's standards, see how this Indian man functions in a white society, and towards the end of the book have him return to an Indian community. ("Baltimore Interview")

## NARRATIVE POINT OF VIEW

As in every novel except *Winter in the Blood*, the story of Welch's fourth novel is told from the point of view of a third-person narrator. *The Indian*

*Lawyer* is different from standard point of view, though, because it begins
with the perceptions of the villain rather than those of the hero. The reader
is introduced to the complexities of plot and character through the voice
of Jack Harwood, a convict serving time at the state penitentiary. Harwood, we learn in the first paragraph, had been knifed a year earlier by
an Indian. Wanting revenge, but also wanting to get out of jail, he plots
to blackmail the one Indian on the parole board, Sylvester Yellow Calf.

The Indian lawyer does not even appear until the middle of the first
chapter. He is described, through the eyes of the convict, as a well-dressed
and handsome man. "Harwood had never seen an Indian in a suit and
tie before" (20). Jack tells the parole board his rehearsed story—why he
had become a criminal, why he had attempted to escape. The first chapter
ends with Jack directing his wife, Patti Ann, to approach the Indian.

At the beginning of Chapter 2, there is a decisive alteration in point of
view. The perspective shifts from Jack's diatribe against Indians to the
centrality of the Indian lawyer, Sylvester Yellow Calf, the man in the suit
and tie who periodically sits in judgment of Jack and the other inmates.
The narrative moves from the inside or prison atmosphere, represented
by both the convict and the parole board, to the outside. Glad to leave his
thoughts about the prisoners behind, Yellow Calf starts thinking about
unrelated matters: the woman he is dating, his clothes, his political future.

Yellow Calf agrees to interview Harwood's wife, who, using an assumed name, pretends that she needs a lawyer. The unsuspecting lawyer
sleeps with her, and through their passion he is caught up in a web of
intrigue, having unknowingly compromised his position on the parole
board in his affair with a convict's wife. After Patti Ann confesses her role
in the blackmail plot, Yellow Calf is forced to confront his actions and
question his judgment. He resigns from the parole board and from the
Congressional race. In typical Welchian style the narrative constantly
shifts gears—from the prison to the law firm to the reservation to the
bedroom to the past.

Welch presents the inside or prison world of Jack through phone calls,
conversations with other convicts, visits, and the interaction between Jack
and two former cons. In a narrative within the narrative, the two partners
in crime scheme to ruin Yellow Calf and to locate Jack's stash from an
earlier robbery. But their plan backfires after the Indian announces his
decision to resign his candidacy for public office. The novel ends at the
Little Flower Catholic Church in Browning, where Yellow Calf, now working for Indian water rights on the Standing Rock reservation in North
Dakota, has come home to attend his grandfather's funeral. He is alone.

The seductive wife and her malicious husband are out of his life. Patti Ann, through the narrative agency of a letter, has written Yellow Calf to tell him that she is waiting patiently for Jack to be paroled.

Whereas at the beginning of the novel Yellow Calf is introduced through the eyes of Jack, at the end he is fixed through the vision of Lena Old Horn, Yellow Calf's former high school counselor. Seeing a tall man filled with "beauty and grace," she pulls her car off the road and watches his delicate moves (349). Intent on his game, Yellow Calf does not see her or the ominous sleet coming from the north. There is a great distance between them. When asked about Lena during the Baltimore interview Welch said, "We know what will happen with the Indian woman, but at this point I think he wants to get back to an Indian community." Although the reader doesn't really "know" what will happen between Yellow Calf and Lena Old Horn, it is conceivable that their separation is temporary and that, like Fools Crow and Red Paint before them, they will form a lasting relationship in an altered world.

## STRUCTURE

In the preceding chapters I use the structure of the vision quest as a way to identify the underlying design of Welch's novels. In *The Indian Lawyer*, however, the term "vision quest" is not applicable, or at least not for Welch's protagonist. Yellow Calf is a modern, assimilated Indian for whom the concepts of relationship to the natural world and the vision quest are drastically modified. The "New Indian," he has already arrived at his destination through a series of trials that have brought him from the basketball court in Browning to a fashionable law firm in Helena. His victory as a basketball player retains some ethnic significance; among many tribes the popular game has replaced the horse raiding and buffalo hunting that were proof of Blackfeet manhood in *Fools Crow*. Yet in the process of being accepted among the white middle class, Yellow Calf represses his memories of the past, losing his ties to his Blackfeet ancestors and to the community.

*The Indian Lawyer* seems to derive its structure, as well as its point of view, from what might be called the parole officer's perspective. Welch's personal experience—he served time on the Montana Board of Pardons in Missoula—makes him particularly aware of the sort of judgmental behavior expected from his central character. Welch, though not a lawyer, knew enough about Montana history and had enough prominence in the larger community to be appointed to the position. As one of the few Indian

members at the top of the prison hierarchy, Welch could readily charac-
terize Yellow Calf, another successful Blackfeet, and how he must feel
about his power over other lives.

Another structural element applied to Welch's novels in other chapters
is the return. The return in *The Indian Lawyer* seems to lack the traditional
meaning that it has in *Fools Crow* and in the Blackfeet narratives recorded
by Henry Bird Grinnell and other ethnographers. Yellow Calf returns to
the Blackfeet reservation periodically, for expected visits and, finally, for
his grandfather's funeral. The return in *The Indian Lawyer* can best be
described as a "troubled homecoming" (Silberman 1989, 101). As in *Winter
in the Blood* and *Fools Crow,* the homecoming is unresolved. In Welch's
words, he is "leaving it ambiguous" as to whether Yellow Calf is returning
to the reservation with total conviction or "if it's partly a retreat from the
white world" ("Baltimore Interview"). But Yellow Calf shows little certainty at the end of the book, so it seems more logical to interpret the
ending as a retreat from both worlds, the white and the Blackfeet.

## PLOT DEVELOPMENT

The basic dynamics of the plot are simple: Jack, a clever criminal, wants
parole. When he is up for review, Yellow Calf and the Montana Board of
Pardons refuse to grant parole. Jack, who hates Indians, orders his wife
to communicate with Yellow Calf, hoping to blackmail the respectable
young attorney. He also contacts two friends from the outside to help in
his blackmail scheme.

Yellow Calf has a girlfriend, Shelley, the divorced daughter of old Senator Hatton. Shelley is "warm, gracious, aristocratic," (49), absolutely no
match for the steamy Patti Ann. It is no surprise when the Indian lawyer
and the convict's wife become feverishly attracted to each other. Mean-
while, the partners in crime scheme to ruin Yellow Calf by kidnapping
Patti Ann. In a legal argument that reveals his own self-interest, Yellow
Calf contacts the parole officer in charge of one of the crooks and plans
to use his political position to threaten him. The blackmailers back down
because the exposed lawyer has already decided to resign from the parole
board and from the Congressional race, rendering their plan meaningless.
To avoid the potential scandal, Yellow Calf withdraws both from the
moral conflict and from the political arena, moving his commitment away
from the state capital to the Standing Rock reservation in North Dakota.

Another aspect of plot focuses on Yellow Calf's conflict between being
an eminent politician and being a spokesman for Indian affairs, where he

might "make a difference" (193). Although he clearly enjoys the attention he is getting from white politicians, being in their company often makes him feel uneasy. At the same time he is uncomfortable at a political rally when an Indian boy hands him a peace pipe; Yellow Calf fears that some members of the Indian Alliance might see him as an "opportunist" who had suddenly adopted Blackfeet customs (295).

Like the story line of Welch's first novel, *Winter in the Blood, The Indian Lawyer* ends with a funeral, a plot device Welch employs both to bring his protagonist home and to place him in a serious situation in which he reviews the past and projects the future. The novel ends ambiguously, with Welch leaving Yellow Calf's options open. Will he run for office again when he is more in control of his emotions? Or practice law somewhere else? Or perhaps stay on the reservation? Because of his cultural alienation throughout the novel, the last choice seems the least likely.

## GENRE

*The Indian Lawyer* is a novel of adventure, a novel of character, a romance, a novel of suspense, a psychological study, and a would-be best seller. It is also a prison novel in reverse. In an inventive change of literary convention, Welch presents his case through a set of ironic contrasts between the Indian lawyer and the white underdog, the one who in ordinary circumstances would win the reader's sympathy. From *The Birdman of Alcatraz* to *Papillon*, to *Soul on Ice*, prison literature has dramatized the hero–convict and his contempt for the Big House. Usually the reader shares in the convict's quest for freedom through release or escape. If there is any kind of quest in *The Indian Lawyer*, it appears to be the convict's and not the lawyer's, Jack's and not Yellow Calf's. The quest is not for valor, as in the Blackfeet tales, but for liberty, as in prison literature.

It has been argued that prison literature is a direct descendant of the African American slave narrative (Lupton 1998, 37–39). The two forms share many themes, including self-education, physical and mental abuse, and the longing to escape confinement. In African American literature the prison narrative became popular during the Civil Rights movement of the 1960s, through the writings of George Jackson, Eldridge Cleaver, Angela Davis, Malcolm X, and other spokespersons. The 1960s and 1970s also brought some striking examples of prison literature from white writers, among them Norman Mailer and Malcolm Braly. Mailer's *The Executioner's Song* (1979) won the 1980 Pulitzer Prize for its portrayal of Gary Gilmore, the convict who refused to fight his death sentence. Former convict Malcolm Braly wrote five prison books, the best known being *On the Yard* (1967) and *False Starts* (1977). Both Cleaver and Braly documented their lives from the inside, from Folsom, San Quentin, and other prisons. Rather than trying selfishly to improve his own situation, as is the case with Jack, Eldridge Cleaver used his time in prison reading the works of Karl Marx and Vladimir Ilyich Lenin to learn how to free his race from white oppression. *Soul on Ice* (Cleaver 1968) attacks the white woman, depicting her as an ogre with claws dug into the Black man's chest. As offensive as Cleaver's image may be, it seems all too true of Patti Ann, who willfully crosses the culturally imposed barriers against interracial sexuality to blackmail Yellow Calf, a minority male.

Malcolm Braly's unforgettable self-portrait in *False Starts* is a lot like Welch's study of Harwood. Jack is a burglar and felon, someone who views the parole board with cynicism. Braly goes from reform school to prison when he is picked up for repeated burglary and attempted escape. His parole board is the Adult Authority, or AA, a three-man infrastructure like Welch's Montana Board of Pardons. During his hearing he is expected to admit that he has a problem: "And no matter what your private opinion, when the Adult Authority, the remote body authorized to grant parole, asked in tones of high seriousness if you had come to grips with your problem, you were willing to concede that you had a problem even if you had to invent one on the spot" (Braly 1976, 158). Jack's reaction to the parole board is similar. He is expected to show remorse: "Remorse, that was the key" (18). When Jack's wife reads the words "Parole denied, pass to discharge of sentence," she is struck by the "clinical, dispassionate language" of the statement (32). The Board of Pardons is the institution with the final say in whether the prisoner stays in or gets out. As Jack hates the Indian lawyer, so Braly hates the one Black man on his parole board: "The black, as he would have had to have been then, was the smartest, as well as the most liberal, but he was also infamous for chewing out his own [people]" (196). Seen from the eyes of the prisoner, a parole board member of any color might be public enemy number one.

Given the popularity of prison literature, and given the reader's tendency to side with the victim, Welch's placement of a parole board member at the center of his novel takes on peculiar dimensions. In *The Indian Lawyer*, the reader is expected to sympathize with an easily duped man in power who has sex several times a week with a woman whose husband is manipulating the scene from behind bars. Welch's novel appears to reverse the racial stereotype in which "The Man," or the white male, usually sits in judgment, imprisoning blacks, Indians, and other racial minorities in ghettos, reservations, and houses of detention. Instead, it is the Indian lawyer who sits in judgment, denying Jack his parole and inciting his hatred. The world of law and order in Welch's fourth novel is apparently upside-down, with the reader expected to root for the wrong person, much like Welch as a child rooted for John Wayne against the Indians (*Native American Novelists Series* 1999). In terms of racial identity, Sylvester Yellow Calf in no way deserves the compassion the reader feels for the jailed Sioux leader Leonard Peltier in *Prison Writings: My Life Is My Sun Dance* (1999) or for Crazy Horse, the imprisoned Sioux warrior of Welch's own *Killing Custer* (1994).

It is urgent to emphasize, though, that the Indian lawyer is not a cowboy but an Indian. If Yellow Calf were a white lawyer with similar economic advantages and a similar political appointment, he would be a very unloved character indeed. But Yellow Calf is an Indian lawyer with an Indian name, the brainchild of an Indian writer. If he has power, he has failed to use it in a politically correct manner, as a way to improve the lives of American Indians. Because he lacks self-knowledge, the Indian lawyer loses control over his fate. He is forced to resign as a Congressional candidate and, subsequently, as a member of the parole board. His press agents cover up for him, reporting that Yellow Calf is redefining his commitments and planning to work with reservation Indians. These commitments seem like an easy way out of a difficult situation.

## CHARACTER DEVELOPMENT

Because *The Indian Lawyer* lacks the grander notions of tribal identity and ethnic survival that had informed Welch's earlier works, it is a realistic but somewhat disappointing portrayal of modern life. With the exception of Sylvester Yellow Calf and to some extent Jack Harwood, its characters are types rather than individuals. They interact in what seems to be a confined and staged space, perhaps reflecting the tightness of the prison/parole controversy at the basis of the plot. The characters, whatever their race, seem for the most part to be locked into their expected roles: ambitious Indian, sultry seductress, wealthy senior statesman, crafty criminal. Its elements of staging and character suggest its potential for film adaptation. If *The Indian Lawyer* were ever adapted into film, it would probably have greater impact than it does in its narrative form. In the Baltimore interview, Welch said, "Amazingly enough, almost all of my books have been optioned for film, except for *Fools Crow* and *The Heartsong of Charging Elk*" ("Baltimore Interview").

The following sections introduce the cast of characters.

## The Lawyer

Sylvester Yellow Calf is a handsome young attorney, a former basketball player for the University of Montana and a graduate of Stanford Law School. As a lawyer practicing in the state capital city of Montana, Helena, Yellow Calf serves on the parole board, as Welch himself had done in Missoula for 10 years. Welch wrote *The Indian Lawyer* in part to give his readership a character whose adventures are of a quiet nature, whose validity derives from a new kind of bravery.

Unfortunately, Yellow Calf as a character is rather smug and unlikable. A conservative Democrat, he is caught between serving the Indian community and being a success in the white one. He emulates both Buster Harrington, his law partner, and Shelley's father, Senator Hatton. When Yellow Calf's affair with Patti Ann takes center stage, Shelley is left in the wings. She learns the awful truth only when Yellow Calf reveals it to his political backers. Without showing very much regret, he abandons his political aspirations and also Patti Ann after becoming aware of the true nature of the liaison. Although Yellow Calf shows strength in recognizing the conflict of interest—he is in love with the wife of a convict over whom he holds the power of parole—he seems to accept the knowledge with detachment. His transformation at the end of the novel from the black-mailed victim of a torrid romance to a dedicated servant of his people is too sudden to be entirely convincing, as is the hint of a possible ethnic conversion through his grandmother, to whom he had briefly returned in the middle of the book.

Although Yellow Calf appears to operate as a free agent, he is nevertheless the product of a repressive background, which he has been trying all of his life to escape. Like the photographer–hero of Thomas King's *Medicine River* (1989), he is torn between the desire to succeed, usually attainable only by leaving the reservation, and the desire to return home to reestablish his roots. The Indian community is "where he belongs," Welch indicated in the Baltimore Interview, often talking about his characters as if they were real people making their own decisions instead of his fictional fabrications. A Blackfeet city-dweller, Yellow Calf has tried to prove himself in a legal system that for centuries has undermined the rights of his people through broken treaties and the inequitable distribution of land and minerals. If he is a success, it is a success purchased at the expense of the Blackfeet nation.

Yellow Calf is personally involved in the system. He is a partner in the law firm of Harrington, Lohn and Associates, which in turn is promoting his candidacy for Congress. His being on the parole board gives him "some record in public service" (55). Then the successful lawyer experiences a "sudden fall from grace"(303) as his promising career is threatened. Realizing that public knowledge of his inappropriate behavior will prevent him from winning the election, Yellow Calf resigns. After a nonsexual New Year's Eve with Patti Ann, Sylvester bids farewell, having coincidentally received a job offer to protect Indian water rights in rural North Dakota.

The final scene shows Yellow Calf in Browning, Montana, after his grandfather's funeral. He is alone, shooting basketball, while Lena Old Horn, a beautiful Indian woman and his former high-school guidance counselor, watches from a distance. One critic interprets this scene as having a "near-religious atmosphere" as Yellow Calf reclaims his heritage through a "ritualized athletic activity" (Donahue 1997, 50–51). Perhaps, reading into the symbolism, Yellow Calf is about to experience a more meaningful life, inspired by the death of his grandfather and by the sacred hoop. On the other hand, the basketball hoop is also a symbol of his aloneness, an empty O. Yellow Calf is alone, without a team, without a woman. He is literally playing with himself. Readers open to a psychological interpretation would see this final shot as a fairly obvious image for masturbation. Sidner Larson's comment about Yellow Calf's capacity to "handle things" without needing women further reinforces his aloneness (1994, 503–04).

Whereas the first of these assessments of character seems too solemn, the second is too severe. The Indian lawyer is not prone to any flaws except for sexual appetite, self-deception, and gullibility, characteristics he shares with most modern Americans. He is, as Hans Bak claims, "a protagonist caught up in the ironic ambiguities of intercultural conflict" (Bak 1995, 35). Furthermore, an Indian lawyer has every right to be moderate, just as an Indian novelist has every right to present an unsympathetic character, as Welch surely did in *The Death of Jim Loney*.

In the last sentence of the novel, Welch suggests that his protagonist is, like Loney before him, playing a losing game: "He was going one on one against the only man who ever beat him" (349). Yellow Calf is a good role model with an imperfect personality. He is a far more enviable Indian than Loney, with a real chance to overcome his disadvantages. Unfortunately, his desire to be a part of the power structure leaves him prey to its manipulations. There is no way, as a representative of authority, that he can avoid contradictions. In the judgment of David Seals, the author of *Powwow Highway*, Welch's novel is "slick and sympathetic, just like the main character" (1990, 648).

## The Criminal

Law and order are what make Jack so interesting a criminal and Yellow Calf so gullible a victim. Jack is a criminal with multiple felonies and two armed robberies. He had escaped from prison and been recaught. He is a specific type of criminal, an intellectual who spends time in the library— reading, shelving books, and plotting his escape. He describes himself as "bright and clean-cut," with degrees in bookkeeping and economics (16). Jack has been an Indian hater even before a hostile Indian knifes him while he is working in the library. An accountant by trade, Jack comes from a wealthy family, in contrast to Yellow Calf, who has risen to his privileged status from poverty. Jack is a middle-class, white-collar culprit. In *False Starts*, Malcolm Braly describes the Jack breed of criminal, the "clean crook," usually a safecracker, who was highly respected on the inside, since he had never had to "disgrace himself by working for wages" (Braly 1977, 124). Jack perfectly fits this formula. One prisoner tells him, "You look like you should be teaching school or being a lawyer" (85). One reviewer particularly admires Welch for his depiction of prison life, of the "convict psyche," and of the hardships of "prison widows" (Parins 1991, 28). In his review of the novel, Sidner J. Larson also commends Welch's "realistic and vivid imaging of the prison setting" (Larson 1991, 65).

When he first introduces Jack, Welch characterizes him as a rather humane criminal who had spent his stolen money paying for his wife's hysterectomy. As the novel progresses, both the point of view and the reader's loyalty shifts from Jack to Yellow Calf, from white man to Indian. Whatever feelings the reader may have had for Jack quickly dissipate as Welch reveals his narrow mind and racial bigotry.

## The Henchmen

Woody Peters and Bobby Fitzgerald, a homosexual couple, are con artists out on suspended sentences. Welch is careful in his treatment of homosexuality in prisons, balancing the reality of prison rape with a rather subtle and sensitive portrayal of the Peters–Fitzgerald relationship. Yellow Calf is surprised to realize that Fitzgerald, despite his Irish name, is part Indian (251).

The Indian lawyer uses his power on the parole board to gather information on Jack's partners in crime. In a suspenseful scene he disguises himself and, taking Patti Ann's Honda instead of his Saab, Yellow Calf goes to the Shanty, a hangout for local criminals, to spy on them. When he finds an empty bottle of cheap bourbon on the front seat of the Honda, he realizes that his detective act has been discovered. The entire blackmail scheme falls apart when Yellow Calf, fearing that the ex-cons might harm Patti Ann, gives up the race for Congress.

## The Anglo Girlfriends

Patti Ann has been unlucky in love. She has had four miscarriages and a hysterectomy during her nine years of marriage, seven spent while her husband was in jail. It is little wonder that her initial conniving to win Yellow Calf's affections soon results in a true romance. After they have sex, Patti Ann exclaims, "My God, my God. It was so good" (151).

In this ethno-detective tale, Yellow Calf is also involved with another white woman, Shelley, a college graduate, the daughter of Senator Hatton and the divorced mother of two daughters. Yellow Calf seems headed for a middle-class marriage and a comfortable lifestyle like his potential father-in-law's until he abandons the educated Shelley for the voluptuous Patti Ann; but not before Welch describes a weekend Yellow Calf and Shelley spend at a spa outside of Helena, where Shelley writes postcards and her lover reminisces about his basketball past and discusses the possibility that he might run for Congress (99–129).

Both of the white women characters are initially disturbed by Yellow Calf's being an Indian. Shelley has trouble imagining that she could have anything "in common" with him (116); Patti Ann has changed from "hating Indians—as an act of loyalty to her husband—to sleeping with one" (152). Both women change their racist attitudes when Yellow Calf wins them over. A feminist might argue, as I do in Chapter 7 of this book, that in *The Indian Lawyer* and in *The Heartsong of Charging Elk*, Welch himself falls prey to racial and sexual stereotyping, in ways that are essential to his plots but that leave the reader feeling aggravated that his male characters are so easily destroyed by white women.

## The Good Indian Woman

Despite the prominent role played by white women in *The Indian Lawyer*, Yellow Calf has long been enamored with Indian women. He recalls that Dolores Bullshoe, an Indian girl from junior high, had been "his first real girlfriend" (233). While he was at Stanford he had an affair with a

Laguna Pueblo woman (128). And there were others. But throughout the novel there is one Indian woman, Lena Old Horn, who serves as a symbol for the kind of relationship that Yellow Calf could have had were it not for his political ambitions and his various relationships. Intelligent, attractive, and six years older than Yellow Calf, she had once been his guidance counselor. After years of separation, the two friends meet again at the end of the novel, where Lena, a Crow, has been working at the Blackfeet reservation in Browning. Lena is Yellow Calf's dream of Indianness: In high school he had visualized her "a hundred years ago in buckskins and shawl doing bead work or dancing a grass dance with other women" (111). Even though Indian women have long been doing grass dances and wearing shawls at the Browning powwow and at Crow Fair in eastern Montana, Yellow Calf protects himself by placing his fantasy of Lena in the distant past. Welch's romanticization of Lena and of the culture she represents is evidence of the Indian lawyer's alienation from a continuing tradition.

## The Elders

Yellow Calf hates both his parents, who have deserted him. He is reared by his Blackfeet grandparents. In high school he senses that he is not connected to his heritage, although he attends naming ceremonies and other events. The elders treat him with "kindness and respect"; still, he feels "distant" from the old people and their rituals (110). His success as basketball player, student, and lawyer has left him further severed from the elders of Browning and their traditions.

His grandfather, Earl Yellow Calf, eventually gives up the traditions, but his grandmother, Mary Bird, continues to attend the powwows, having experienced a renewed cultural commitment in her mid-forties after having been a "flapper," a word used in the 1920s for a woman who was considered "bold or unconventional" (*Webster's New World Dictionary*). Neither of the grandparents can sustain an influence on Sylvester Yellow Calf, whose journey to the city marks his separation from family and community.

### STYLE AND LITERARY DEVICES

The style in *The Indian Lawyer* varies from the middle-class diction of a Stanford Law School graduate to the street language of the hardened criminal, with all the obscenities intact. Ron McFarland calls it a "rather racy and gritty book" (McFarland 2000, 139). Welch is especially effective in giving voice to the novel's scoundrel, Jack. Jack's wife, Patti Ann, tends to think and speak in the clichés of romance fiction. During her first sexual encounter with Yellow Calf, "she guided him into her and saw his large brown hands kneading her white breasts" (152). Although Welch had used erotic language effectively in *Fools Crow,* it seems awkward and overdone in *The Indian Lawyer,* as if Welch were straining to satisfy a public raised on romance fiction. Ron McFarland excuses Patti Ann's triteness, arguing that Welch "intends for the sentiments and their expression to match the character" (McFarland 2000, 131).

Welch is for the most part an expert when it comes to the use of dialog. He has clearly mastered the narrative techniques of popular fiction, creating conversations within the text to convey the distinctive language of his characters, something he does more consistently in *The Indian Lawyer* than in any of his other novels. He adeptly moves into the mind of his central character, using simple descriptive tags to display Yellow Calf's legal insights. Like many members of his profession, Yellow Calf has the ability to think aloud. If there is any word used most often in the novel, it is some form of the verb "to think."

In addition to establishing dialog as a form of external and internal communication, Welch relies on certain standard devices from detective fiction, including tough-guy talk, prison slang, and the building up of suspense. He also effectively bridges the gap between the oral tradition of *Fools Crow* and the print culture of *The Indian Lawyer,* including some of the mythological and historical language of Blackfeet religion—Sun Chief (220), "Cold Maker" (166), the ancient narratives, the "Massacre on the Marias" (155). But the lawyer views his tradition with detachment, approaching it through maps and books, "the way a hobbyist or academic would" (156).

David Seals, though he objects to the book for its failure to convey the Native American oral tradition, concedes that Welch's prose is "recognizably competent and polished" (Seals 1990, 648). Edward Hoagland finds his style to be "apt" and "mature" (Hoagland 1990, 7). There is no doubt that Welch's fourth novel shows a development in novelistic skills, especially in the use of dialog. But it lacks the depth of *Winter in the Blood,* the angst of *The Death of Jim Loney,* and the profound vision of *Fools Crow.*

## SETTING

In *The Indian Lawyer,* the vast Montana landscape of Welch's former settings has been mostly reduced to an urban center, the state capital Helena, where Yellow Calf practices law. The novel is set in the present (1988–

89). It contains references to the politics of the day, as Democrats from Montana work for political change and gain following the Reagan–Bush years (204). Much of the setting is inside—in the prison, at the parole hearing, in Harrington's library, in Sylvester's bedroom. Getting out of the city means going to Chico Hot Springs, where Shelley exclaims, "I could live here forever, breathing this mountain air, swimming, eating in that wonderful dining room" (99).

Only during Yellow Calf's long drives through the prairies does Welch furnish eloquent descriptions of setting, reminding the reader of the lush passages in *Winter in the Blood* and *Fools Crow*. The landscape emerges at unanticipated moments, such as when Yellow Calf drives his Saab to visit his grandparents, commutes to his new job at the Standing Rock Reservation in North Dakota, or when he remembers his childhood in Browning. Significantly, when he represents the Sioux at Standing Rock, he lives in a rented apartment in Bismarck, North Dakota, a city of about 50,000 people that is an hour and a half's drive from the work site. His distance from the reservation accentuates his isolation; it also affords Welch with a device for recording what his character thinks and sees while in motion.

Although animals are still an essential aspect of setting, they appear primarily on the horizon, observed when Yellow Calf leaves the city or when he looks back to his reservation past. Seeing the "occasional animal"—a badger, a hawk, a prairie dog, an antelope—helps him to remember the prairie even when he is far away (158). There are also a few references to pet cats and dogs, along with the surprise appearance of a puppy (328), introduced but for some reason never explained. On New Year's Eve Yellow Calf imagines "a dark bird, ever present, circling slowly over the festivities" (338). The bird symbol, so prevalent in *The Death of Jim Loney*, is not developed in *The Indian Lawyer*. If these fragmented images have any effect at all, it is in their emphasis on the absence of relationship between Yellow Calf and the animal world. There is always some barricade between him and nature, usually the windshield of his "dark green Saab" (157). The greenness of the protected car seems to separate him from the green mountain ranges and Montana's Big Sky.

## THEMATIC ISSUES

### Sports

As observed in the chapter on *The Death of Jim Loney*, Welch refers to sports in all of his novels, often using the sports arena as a way of developing theme and character. Sports can have a binding effect on players and fans. In explaining a special exhibition of Indian toys and games at the Mitchell Museum of the American Indian, curator Janice Klein said that indigenous people used games for both amusement and training. For the Indian, games had a spiritual aspect and embodied the idea that players do not specialize, which is why they haven't usually stood out as stars. Winning basketball teams in Montana frequently prefer star quilts to trophies in recognition of victory, thus verifying their heritage (Klein 2002). Sidner J. Larson affirms the centrality of basketball in *The Indian Lawyer:* "The Indian has taken back basketball from the whites and made it into a way of continuing traditional ways" (Larson 1991, 66).

It is possible that basketball has its origins in the Native American game hoop-and-pole (Oxendine 1988, 58–60). Competitive games were an aspect of Indian life long before the white man came, and their effects are felt in contemporary life and literature. "Though Indians constituted but 7 per cent of Montana's population, their schools would win ten Class A, B, and C state high school titles between 1980 and 1990" (Smith 1992, 5). In Larry Colton's novel *Counting Coup* (2001), basketball is an aspect of communal support that connects contemporary players to their origins; it equates the Indian tradition of touching the enemy in battle to the rivalry between a Montana women's basketball team and their white opponents.

For Sylvester Yellow Calf games have a far-reaching implication. He escapes the reservation and enters a white-dominated environment by becoming a star basketball player. Basketball in his case is a means to an end rather than a communally shared spiritual journey. When a white reporter singles him out as the star player, Yellow Calf becomes alienated from the others on his team. This alienation continues as Yellow Calf races down the court—from high school to Division One basketball at the University of Montana to a scholarship at Stanford Law School. "The more successful he becomes at basketball and beyond, and the more recognition he receives for his achievements, the further he distances himself from his people and heritage" (Donahue 1997, 49).

## Tradition

Another of Welch's themes is Blackfeet tradition, symbolized by the medicine pouch. In *Winter in the Blood,* the unnamed narrator throws his grandmother's medicine pouch into the open grave, suggesting the end of Blackfeet ritual; in *Fools Crow* the pouch, handed down to Heavy Shield Woman by her predecessor, represents the cultural continuity of the Blackfeet nation. The medicine bag has several implications in *The Indian Law-yer*. On his first visit to see his grandparents, Yellow Calf thoughtlessly (or perhaps intentionally) leaves the pouch, given to him by his grand-mother, in his room before returning to the city. Later, during a political rally, the reader learns that Yellow Calf has taken the war medicine with him, feeling that its presence makes him "aggressive and confident" (293). In another scene he contemplates the meaning of his great-great-grandfather's medicine dangling from a mirror. When Yellow Calf returns for the funeral, Mary Bird, nearly blind, laughs at her reflected image when she notices that the pouch is no longer in the bureau. The medicine bag thus represents Yellow Calf's tentative return to his ancestors but at the same time a rejection of its magic. It is more of a cultural "archive" than a spiritual object (293).

## The New Warrior

In keeping with the theme of tradition is the emergence of a third theme, the New Warrior, often a lawyer, who replaces his predecessors on a dif-ferent battlefield. The New Warrior can be characterized as an Indian who knows his or her tribal rights and ancestry and who, through education, legal action, the writing of literature, and other forms of engagement as-serts those rights in the process of reclaiming a continent. According to Welch, "Lawyers are the quintessential New Indians. In the Indian com-munity lawyers are called the New Warriors. I thought Yellow Calf would be a good character to represent the new, successful Indians" ("Baltimore Interview").

There are several references to the New Warrior in the text. When Yel-low Calf is in high school his guidance counselor, Lena Old Horn, gives him an article on the New Warriors that advises water law as a viable career choice (106). Although at times Yellow Calf fears that he has failed his cultural mission, he finds gratification working on the North Dakota reservation. In a long paragraph packed with legal specifics, he thinks about the "small triumph" in getting the circuit court to set a date for the hearings, and he promises himself to take the water rights case "to wher-ever it ended," possibly to the Supreme Court. Giving up his partnership had started to feel like a "small sacrifice" (342–343).

In September 2002 I interviewed a tribal elder, a Cherokee woman named Medicine Warrior. She attributed the legal profession with the strides in Indian advances during the past several decades, pointing out the 1963 Education Act, so that Native Americans could begin to learn their language; the 1978 Native American Religious Freedom Act; and the 1992 passage of the Native American Great Protection Act, which is intended to return confiscated land to the tribes. Medicine Warrior insisted that although it wasn't the general public who made the laws, "the laws are what governs our lives."

For the laws to change one needs lawyers, because Native Americans are not allowed tribal representation in the House of Representatives or the Senate. Within this context, Yellow Calf's desire to make a difference through Congressional representation is a partial fulfillment of Medicine Warrior's need for a changed legal system, although he would be at a far greater advantage if he could run for the Blackfeet seat in the United States Congress. It is important that both Medicine Woman, and, to a lesser degree, Yellow Calf have used their advantages of education and social awareness in their work as New Warriors.

The three themes outlined here are combined in an introspective scene in which Yellow Calf holds the medicine pouch and looks in the mirror, trying to imagine himself as a Blackfeet warrior. But he sees instead a disheveled man whose "only war, skirmish, actually, was with himself" (168). The phrasing in this fragment is important, for it foreshadows the solitary basketball game of the last sentence, in which Yellow Calf competes against "the only man who ever beat him"—himself (349). The word *skirmish* means a short conflict or battle. It is also a sports term relevant to football, rugby, and fencing. In his own desperate war/game, Yellow Calf plays alone, with no teammate, against a mirrored image. Holding his ancestor's medicine pouch against his neck, he regards himself in the mirror and realizes that he "wasn't even a new warrior. He was a fat cat warrior, helping only himself, and some fatter cats, get richer" (167–168).

## ALTERNATIVE READING: MARXIST CRITICISM

Marxist or dialectical criticism is an approach to literature grounded in the relationship between the art object and the social order that surrounds it. Marxist theory has its roots in the political and cultural analyses of Karl Marx (1818–1883) and Friedrich Engels (1820–1895). It operates on certain assumptions: that "reality" can be ascertained; that social and economic values shape our convictions; that through class struggle we can realize a society in which all people have an equal opportunity (Bressler 2003, 162).

Marxist literary theory is an application of the economic theories of Marx and Engels to the literary production, based on the "understanding of art itself as a commodity" (Groden and Kreiswirth 1994, 491). Some of its major proponents have been the Hungarian critic Georg Lukacs (1885–1971), Frederic Jameson in the United States, Terry Eagleton in England, and a score of other critics who analyze literature in terms of class, society, language, economics, and culture (Murfin 2003, 379).

It is the function of the Marxist critic to demonstrate the interrelationship between prevailing beliefs and literary forms and to point to the basic contradictions between social ideals and novelistic patterns. As Raman Selden emphasizes, "dialectical criticism does not isolate individual literary works for analysis; an individual is always part of a larger structure (a tradition or a movement) or part of a historical situation" (Selden 1989, 45).

*The Indian Lawyer*, then, should be viewed within the political context of Welch's work and within the larger historical perspective. Even in a novel that deals with contemporary issues, Welch includes numerous references to the Marias Massacre (1870), a historical event that he continuously invokes in his fiction. In *The Indian Lawyer*, Yellow Calf recalls the event while driving on the interstate, having taken a theoretical interest in Blackfeet history (155). By evoking the Marias Massacre in his novels and nonfiction, Welch locates the disaster within a broadly based cultural frame that includes its impact on the Blackfeet tribal economy, its impact on the survivors, its effect on the author's memory, and its consequences for a contemporary American Indian ideology.

In addition to examining the historical context of a work of fiction, a Marxist critic analyzes its social pyramid, relating his or her observations to a theory of class structure. "Marxism declares that in America the capitalists hold the economic purse strings, and because they do, they control the base, making the capitalists the center of power" (Bressler 2003, 171). The lowest social class or base in *The Indian Lawyer* is the reservation Indian. The Pine Ridge reservation of South Dakota is in Shannon County, the poorest county in the United States (Brokaw 2000, 1). Denied a decent job, often living without electricity or a telephone, the Indian in many areas of the country subsists on a level barely above poverty. In his poetry and in his earlier novels *Winter in the Blood* and *The Death of Jim Loney*, Welch has depicted Indians who resort to alcohol as a solution to their social problems. In the mid-1970s, social workers in the Seattle Indian Alcoholism Program realized that "over ninety percent of the Indians in jails and prisons in the state of Washington were there for alcohol-related offences" (Little Rock 1989, 9).

A Marxist would argue that the prison is an extension of the reservation, an additional place to impound those who do not comply with the ide-

ology of the ruling class. The modern prison has its own hierarchical structure: At the top is the governor, next is the parole board, and at the bottom
is the prisoner locked in the isolation pit or "hole," with intermittent levels
such as wardens, trustees, psychiatrists, and guards, all of whom divert
the function of the judge, who is no longer "purely and simply he who
punishes" (Foucault 1995, 22). The prison jobs are also stratified. A former
accountant, Jack gets the soft jobs such as bookkeeping and library services. He is a "clean crook," what Malcolm Braly calls "the aristocrat of
the criminal class" (124).

In contrast are the Indians, the blacks, and the Mexicans, who work
outside in the dairy (12). With the possible exception of the weekly sweat
lodge at Leavenworth prison in Kansas, Indian prisoners have been consistently denied their spiritual rights and rituals. They have argued that
prison officials have no knowledge of the Indian way of life and worship
(see Peltier 2000, 183–190; Little Rock 1989, 9; and Sanchez 2003, 1). Sylvester Yellow Calf, despite his heritage, shows little empathy for Indian
prisoners. Rather, he puts them out of his mind when the parole hearings
are over, wanting to forget the "paint-sniffing, brain-fried Indians who
hadn't had any opportunities, any chance" (39).

Yellow Calf, caught in a class struggle between rich and poor, white
and Indian, escapes the reservation in Browning by playing the game of
basketball. Later, as a lawyer and potential candidate for Congress, he
aspires to the ruling class; at the same time he wants to represent the
Blackfeet people, to change things. He is a character caught up in the
"paradoxes of assimilation" (Back cover, *The Indian Lawyer*). Yellow Calf's
rise from poverty to a seat on the state Board of Pardons could be interpreted as a triumphant overthrowing of racial and economic barriers, one
that duplicates Welch's own ethnic achievements as a Blackfeet Indian.

In his multi-ethnic application of class contradictions, Welch provides
a political novel with clear sociological implications and with almost no
jargon. *The Indian Lawyer* lends itself to a mild form of Marxist critique of
the kind that has challenged orthodox Marxist criticism since the 1960s,
when "movements such as feminism and ethnic studies" began to provide
a multidimensional reading of class conflict (Groden and Kreiswirth 1994,
499).

Readers who advocate a more radical approach to America's ethnic
problems will perhaps be disappointed by Welch's mild-mannered attorney. Yellow Calf is a moderate brand of lawyer, a dim shadow of the
American Indian Movement (AIM) warriors who have used legal expertise and radical protest in their efforts to extricate their people from op-

pression. Welch admitted that his central character is "not radicalized at all. He wants to do the right thing by everybody" ("Baltimore Interview").

Sylvester Yellow Calf represents the rising Indian middle class, whereas Buster Harrington, head of Harrington, Lohn and Associates, represents the capitalist. Welch describes the Harrington mansion in lavish detail. "There was no ballroom, no billiard room, just gracious high-ceilinged rooms trimmed in imported woods and brass sconces and fixtures" (41). He and his wife collect chandeliers and oil paintings. Harrington belongs to the exclusive Montana Club. He urges Yellow Calf to run for Congress, using the images of capitalism in his argument: It will "pay off"; Indians will "reap the benefits" (193).

In recent history Indian people have discovered a way to get their own high-ceilinged rooms and extravagant art. Tribally organized Native Americans have attempted to resolve the differences between the rich and the poor, the propertied and the disenfranchised, by building casinos. When a small tribe dares to construct a gambling complex, there are bound to be loud objections, especially when the casino threatens the real estate held for centuries by settlers. In *Without Reservation* (2000) Jeff Benedict provides an intriguing, if biased, account of how a small band of Mashantucket Pequot Indians used legal and financial expertise to create Foxwoods, the largest casino in the world, and of how the white residents of Ledyard, Connecticut, reacted in disbelief as it was all happening.

In the Baltimore Interview, I asked Welch about casinos, about whether he thought they were helping Indians get back some of what they had lost. He responded that although he had been to only a few casinos, one in Connecticut and one in Minnesota, they might serve some purpose. "Indians are tired of being poor. Now they are doing something for themselves, and a lot of people are coming down on them."

Welch had a number of questions concerning the legitimacy of casinos. "Does that money really filter down to individual Indians? Are good social and educational programs being built as a result of that money? If you went to the Minnesota casino you might ask them, 'What's really happening to this money? Are any of your tribe on welfare? Can all of them go to school and college on this money?'" ("Baltimore Interview").

Because of casinos many Indians have been able to enter the middle class and to insure their communities against a continued legacy of hunger and disease. "Indian gaming is transforming the face of Native America as tribes at last begin to accumulate financial resources to develop businesses, to create modern community infrastructure (from schools and health centers to housing and drinking water systems)—in general—to catch up with the 'American Dream'" (Hill 2003, 46). Indian gaming has become a major weapon in the Indian's struggle to retrieve lost land and lost honor. A Marxist would argue that the astounding increase in Indian casinos not far from large urban populations is a further means of redistributing the wealth.

A final strategy for economic reparation is organized resistance of the kind that AIM conducted in 1969 in its 19-month occupation of Alcatraz Island and in 1973 in its 71-day occupation of Wounded Knee, South Dakota (Wittstock and Salinas, 3–4). Among Indians of the twenty-first century serving time for militancy, the most noted is Leonard Peltier, who was jailed after the alleged shooting of two FBI agents on the Pine Ridge Reservation in June of 1975 and who has spent 30 years in prison without adequate medical care and without parole. In April 2002 he was again denied a fair hearing for clemency and parole. Outcries against his imprisonment have been heard in cities and on reservations throughout the United States; support continues each day through an online petition that in November 2003 had more than 30,500 signatures.

Like Angela Davis and George Jackson, like Crazy Horse and Sitting Bull, Leonard Peltier is a political prisoner. In *Prison Writings*, he describes his life in captivity as "one unending blur of jails and prisons, with occasional visits to courtrooms" (Peltier 2000, 143). What preserves his strength is his belief that his pain has made him a New Warrior. "I will accept my pain, whether inner or outer, as a warrior does, without whining, without whimpering, as we learn to do in Sun Dance" (147). It is Peltier's identification with his heritage that connects him to all humanity. "We are in this together—the rich, the poor, the red, the white, the black, the brown, and the yellow. We are all one family of humankind" (201). It seems that long before Marx and Engels constructed their concept of a classless society, that vision was inherent to Native American thought. "Mitakuye Oyasin, *my Lakota brethren say./We are all related./We are One*" (Peltier 2000, 26, emphasis in original).

# *The Heartsong of Charging Elk* (2000)

Interviews and first drafts have enabled readers of Welch's *The Heartsong of Charging Elk* to understand how he dramatically altered his original vision for the better. Welch told William Bevis in 1995, five years before *Charging Elk* reached the book stores, that his intended narrator was Jack Dawes, great-grandson of an Oglala Sioux and a French woman. Welch imagined Dawes as a type described in *The Indian Lawyer*, a teacher and a writer, someone not involved with the reservation or his people. But when Dawes learns the story of a Sioux who joined the Buffalo Bill Show, he immediately identifies with the narrative. Welch's plan, then, was to create a historical novel within a modern frame ("Wylie Tales: An Interview with James Welch" 1995, 5–6).

An excerpt from Welch's novel in progress, tentatively titled *Marseilles Gracen*, appeared in *Weber Studies* in 1995. Compared to the lively contemporary style of *The Indian Lawyer*, this excerpt is rather clumsy, full of unnecessary details; for instance: "Several planes of all sizes and colors were lined up nose to tail in a wavy haze of exhausted fuel waiting for their turn to take off. Then the plane lifted and drove up into the lighter sky" (N.G.). In a post–9/11 world this description might seem ominous; here it represents excess baggage.

On the flight Jack Dawes dreams of his eight-year old daughter, dead from a bike accident, standing with a naked man. This dream, the accident, the phone call from his father asking for money—all of these matters of plot are eliminated from the final text, as is the entire contemporary framework. What remains is a historical novel, *The Heartsong of Charging Elk*, as sharply chiseled as the memorial to Crazy Horse, north of the town of Custer in the Black Hills of South Dakota. While not quite so powerful a novel as *Fools Crow*, *Charging Elk* is a gripping, intriguing account of Indian ancestry, of what it was like to have been a Sioux living among Europeans at the end of the nineteenth century. The political parallel is obvious; a Sioux Indian transplanted to a strange city, Charging Elk loses his identity, just as his generation of reservation Indians had lost theirs.

## NARRATIVE POINT OF VIEW

*Charging Elk* opens with a prologue. It is told in the past tense by an unidentified third person narrator who, in a saddened and subdued voice, recounts the fate of the Oglala Sioux a year after the battle of Little Bighorn. Red Cloud and a band of Indians have been captured, among them Crazy Horse; a boy of "eleven winters" watches, telling his younger brother and sister not to cry. As they move toward the fort the captive Indians sing the peace song, a song the narrator would remember forever (1–4).

Chapter 1 begins with the protagonist's name, Charging Elk: "*Charging Elk opened his eyes and he saw nothing but darkness*" (5, emphasis in original). His back aches as he drifts in and out of consciousness. There are no words, only thoughts, like the "muddy" thoughts at the beginning of *The Death of Jim Loney*. He hears a language he does not recognize, sees food that is totally foreign to him. Nothing is familiar. He is without a language, without a culture, a "true stranger in a strange land" (Peck 2001, 2). Like Jim Loney, an earlier "stranger" in Welch's fiction, Charging Elk is set apart from his heritage. He is destined to live with his existential isolation rather than to end it, like Loney, in death.

Throughout the novel Welch uses point of view to brilliant effect, engaging the reader in Charging Elk's struggle to gain a new vocabulary and to maintain self-respect in a society that treats him like an alien. Using dreams and flashbacks, Welch communicates his protagonist's thoughts, which change in perspective from self-reflective observation to a gradual interaction with the other characters, all of them French. At the end of the novel the point of view has shifted so radically that Charging Elk is now a French-speaking citizen, whereas the band of Oglala Sioux whom he seeks out and ultimately rejects have become virtual strangers to him.

## PLOT DEVELOPMENT

In *The Heartsong of Charging Elk* James Welch is careful to present two conflicting plots, the original life of an Oglala Sioux and his later existence as a dislocated Indian trapped in France. The first plot, the briefer one, is introduced in the prologue and reiterated at various intervals in the novel. It is concerned with origins, with the homeland that Charging Elk had shared with the Oglala Sioux. The young Charging Elk recounts the Sioux defeat of George Armstrong Custer at the Battle of Little Bighorn, a story that Welch tells with assurance, having already presented the narrative in his awesome 1992 video script with Paul Stekler, *Last Stand at Little Bighorn* and in his 1994 nonfiction work, *Killing Custer.* In both *Killing Custer* and the fictionalized account of Little Bighorn in *The Heartsong of Charging Elk,* the Oglala ancestors are vanquished by invading forces.

Against the chronicle of late nineteenth-century American history the major French plot unfolds. What makes Welch's fifth novel so different from any of his others is that Charging Elk lives in Europe and not in the United States. *The Heartsong of Charging Elk* begins in France, in 1889, after Buffalo Bill and his troupe had performed in Marseilles. Charging Elk, who falls from his horse and is injured, awakens in a hospital in Southern France, alone, desperate to find his countrymen and return home. After "noticing that people only seem to leave the hospital when they die" (Bogenschutz 2000, 155), he escapes and wanders the streets of Marseilles for four days, destitute and hungry, until he is arrested for vagrancy. He is surrounded by white people with a strange and indecipherable language, a situation that is a repetition of what happened to indigenous Americans placed on reservations. He is eventually befriended by the Soulas family, who provide him with work at their fish market and teach him the rudiments of the French language.

When he has saved enough money, Charging Elk moves to his own quarters and gets a job in a soap factory, where he first labors at firing the furnaces and later works his way up to wrapping soap. He begins to emulate the dress of the white Parisians, buying a "tailored suit, a few shirts, and some shiny brown shoes" (233). But when he visits a house of prostitution, something quite common among foreign men in port cities, the civilized world turns against him. Unwisely, Charging Elk falls in love with Marie, a prostitute.

On the very night that Charging Elk plans to propose, Marie agrees to drug her lover so that an old enemy and scoundrel, Monsieur Breteuil, can gain access to him. In the plot's one shocking episode, Charging Elk awakes from his drugged trance to discover that it is not Marie's mouth on his penis but the mouth of Breteuil, the long-time male enemy who had once tried to seduce him. It is the abnormality of the sexual encounter that so provokes the Oglala Sioux, who has been tricked into committing an act that runs against his cultural values. The reader, who has come to accept Charging Elk as almost French, realizes the vastness of the cultural gaps between the naive Indian and his sophisticated tormentor. In horror Charging Elk reverts to the "savagery" expected from an Indian; his self-restraint, his European facade, erupts in an act of Lakota revenge. He stabs his tormenter to death.

As Welch explained, "This incident goes against his culture, this blow job. He has already determined that this guy is *siyoko*. It goes to the culture, it goes to a tabooed act." Enraged, Charging Elk kills the *siyoko* [the Sioux word for evil one] who had so humiliated him ("Baltimore Interview"). Although the Sioux's reaction is perhaps understandable within his own ethnic context, the French were unable to accept the idea of cultural difference. Charging Elk is pronounced guilty and sentenced to life in prison, hopelessly entrapped by the "double-bind of a legal system that does not recognize the principles by which the Lakota live" (Frase 2002, 20).

After the trial Welch tries to make his plot cover too many incidents in too short a time (Bloomstran 2002, 1–2). Charging Elk slowly adjusts to the restrictions of prison life, acting with a flexibility gleaned from his nomadic tribal origins and from his being abandoned by Buffalo Bill. Because of his great success in learning the trade of tree-trimming, he is permitted to work in the prison garden, where he experiences an untroubled sense of being and belonging for the first time since Marie had betrayed him. After serving 10 years he is released to Vincent Gazier, a tree farmer with a young daughter, Nathalie. Charging Elk and Nathalie marry and quit the farm, resettling in Marseilles, a city where, despite the painful memories it holds for him, Charging Elk again finds personal salvation through labor, stamina, and a sense of duty. He also revives an old interest in drawing, recapturing his life on the Plains to his wife's delight.

At the end of the novel, in an ironic act of separation, Welch brings both plots, the Lakota and the European, together. Charging Elk learns that a small band of Oglala Sioux are encamped in Marseilles performing in the Wild West Show on a return tour to France. For days he is distracted, fearing the possibility that his incessant desire to return to his tribe might be answered, although "he didn't want it so much now" (420).

In the concluding episode Welch circles the plot back to its beginnings, unbinding the strands, the European and the Oglala, rather than connecting them. Charging Elk seeks out the performers, addressing them in Lakota. After they exchange greetings, the Indians relay to Charging Elk the story of his family and of his people. They tell him news from home: how they were made to cut their hair and were forbidden to speak Lakota; how his father has died of influenza; how his mother is alone and needs her son. One of the Sioux begs his lost friend to come home. But the heart of Charging Elk has changed after 16 winters of absence. Reluctantly, he refuses and walks away from the group, having made a choice "between past and present, between his old culture and his new culture, between what has been lost and what has been gained" (Miles 2000, 1). The last sentence reads: "He needed to walk and the Moon of the Falling Leaves would light his way" (438).

Some critics have found solace in Welch's conclusion: "But in the end, the book is healing and redemptive, a revelation of the human heart and spirit" (Knickerbocker 2000, 16). The end, however, is not the end. Imitating the circular pattern of the Native American oral tradition, *The Heartsong of Charging Elk* rotates the plot back to its beginnings, in the protagonist's encounter with the Sioux performers. In that confrontation, which is constricted in both words and emotions, the reader again senses Charging Elk's alienation from both the Sioux and European identities. The sacred hoop is broken and Welch's hero, now "thirty-seven winters," has learned to communicate with the French. "My wife is one of them and my heart is her heart," he says, not in jubilation but in acceptance (437).

Nancy Pearl and Jennifer Young, like the majority of the novel's reviewers, assume that the novel is a complete work, one that develops the ideas of "sorrow, longing, and ultimately acceptance" (Pearl and Young 2002, 244). A reviewer for *Native Peoples* writes of the ending: The protagonist is "freed at last from the bondage of aloneness and separation. Thus his fascinating story becomes one not merely of survival but of self-redemption, a challenge and a promise to all who seek a homeland of the spirit and the mind" (Tack 2000, 36).

"Heartsong," Welch's ambivalent title, implies both joy and self-redemption. Yet within the novel there is a prominent disruption, a sense of loss and separation that belies the lyricism. Many critics tend to forget that none of Welch's novels ends in an ultimate way. As he has made clear in frequent interviews, one of his preferred techniques of plot development is to leave the ending ambiguous or unsettled.

The unfinished nature of Welch's endings is most emphatically true of *The Heartsong of Charging Elk.* As of July 2002, Jim and Lois Welch were preparing to leave for France to do research on a sequel ("Montana Interview"). Set in southern France, it would cover the time period prior to the Great War of 1918. Now that Welch has died, one can only speculate about the apparently unfinished sequel. Was the *Weber Studies* excerpt about Jack Dawes and his dead eight-year-old daughter perhaps the beginning of a new book, a recircling from past to present? Did Nathalie die in a bombing in 1918, leaving Charging Elk a widower? At this time there are no answers, although history indicates that Buffalo Bill Cody did not return to France. Cody died in 1917, several decades after his Cowboy and Indian show had lost its popularity.

Welch told us that he planned to return Charging Elk to America, a decision that would fulfill the separation-initiation-return pattern of the Native American oral tradition. He also said that he would like to write another novel with a contemporary setting. He expressed no desire to return to his own beginnings, to the poetry he rode in on ("Montana Interview").

## STRUCTURE

In this book, I have consistently viewed structure within the Native American framework of the vision quest. In that tradition the hero leaves the community to perform acts of bravery, then returns to claim a position of honor so that he can be suitable for marriage and for tribal leadership. Yet because Charging Elk and the Sioux people were culturally uprooted after they were relegated to reservations, the traditional vision quest could not be accomplished. The dislocation is further compounded for Charging Elk, lost in a foreign land where a sense of community is inconceivable. By necessity, his vision quest must be translated into modern terms such as "the notion of exile, the reinvention of self, and the idea of cultural identity" (Methot 2000, 21). Although Welch had explored similar themes in *Winter in the Blood* and *The Death of Jim Loney*, they are more dramatic when silhouetted against an entirely alien environment.

Throughout the novel Charging Elk remembers the customs, the battles, the rituals of his homeland. When he sees a religious procession of men in "golden robes with tall stiff hats" (66), he recalls the Sun Dance, the "holiest ceremony" of the Sioux, forbidden to them when they were placed on reservations but nonetheless practiced, as Charging Elk had himself performed the flesh sacrifice when he was 17 (66–67). He continues to be known as Charging Elk, even though other matters of dress, language, and manners have been accommodated to satisfy European standards. Charging Elk is a stranger in a strange skin, a Native American uprooted from the Plains and cast into a country that has general contempt for his body and his dress, his hair and his speech.

In like fashion, the pattern of return has fresh implications in Welch's fifth novel. Kathleen Sands has described the central motifs of Welch's first three novels: alienation, the quest for self-identity, and the reentry into the Indian community (Sands 1987, 73–85). The last of these, the reentry or return, is unfulfilled in *The Heartsong of Charging Elk*; it is introduced, deliberated upon, longed for, but ultimately denounced. At the end of the novel, when the chance to return to America presents itself as an opportunity, Charging Elk is no longer able to respond to the calls of his Oglala community. The foreign land, his French wife's father's land, is now his. He has become an expatriate. Once a Sioux warrior and now an assimilated Indian, Charging Elk is committed to the French language, to the French way of life, and to a French wife who has become his "heartsong."

Like many of Welch's concepts, *heartsong* reflects both cultures, the French and the Oglala. In terms of Euro-American fiction it indicates his love for Nathalie. For the Sioux it is the "braveheart song" of the elders, sung in farewell as their young men joined Buffalo Bill in Nebraska so many moons ago (345). For readers who have loved Welch's fiction, *heartsong* is a deeply felt farewell from a writer whose "spare, understated prose explored the complex relationship between his origins and the world outside" (Saxon 2003, 1).

## CHARACTER DEVELOPMENT

In the prologue Welch introduces the central character: an unnamed young boy who is captured by the *Wasichu* (or, for the Blackfeet, *Napikwan*) cavalry. Refusing to submit to the reservation, he flees to the Black Hills, to the wilderness of South Dakota. Welch explained, "I did deliberately leave him in the Black Hills instead of going to a reservation school and becoming Christianized like a lot of the others because I wanted this world to be completely strange" ("Baltimore Interview"). Charging Elk, a splendid horseman after his years in the wilderness, accepts the offer to join Buffalo Bill's Wild West Show.

Welch defines the initial conflict of character in the novel as the one between Charging Elk, a Sioux warrior with nothing left of his heritage but memories, and Buffalo Bill Cody, the American capitalist whose Wild West Show imitated the antipathy between Indians and cavalry during the Plains wars. It is Buffalo Bill's absence from the action of the novel that makes him so important to the fate of its hero.

Buffalo Bill (William Cody) was born in a log cabin in Iowa in 1846. A Union soldier in the Civil War, he later became known as a scout for the Fifth Cavalry during the Indian Wars and became one of only four civilians to receive the Medal of Honor. His most notorious exploit was in one-to-one combat with a Cheyenne warrior, Yellow Hand. Cody killed and scalped Yellow Hand, winning himself an international reputation (Fees 1990, 138–46).

A successful businessman who knew what the public wanted, William Cody created a venue for middle class Americans and Europeans willing to pay to see the reenactment of battles from the Plains Wars. The more famous Indian chiefs such as Sitting Bull, Red Cloud, Black Elk, Crazy Horse, and Geronimo were box-office attractions to whites at the turn of the century. Such men of stature were lured into performing for Cody, who "depicted the Indian so negatively and so crassly" (Kilpatrick 1999, 13), for a number of reasons: They knew they were only playacting; they were motivated by the fact of "confinement made worse by hunger;" and they thought they might learn the "secrets" of the whites (Kilpatrick 1999, 13).

The Buffalo Bill Show was one of several venues that helped to foster the conflicting popular images of Indians as "scantily dressed men with feathers in their hair" but also as "calm, wise elders, in full-feathered headdress, models of stoic restraint" (Kasdan and Tarvernetti 1998, 124). During the infamous Battle of Wounded Knee (1890) Buffalo Bill was at the site, maneuvering to hire some of the Indian prisoners to perform in Europe. "The tragedy of the 'Battle' of Wounded Knee became just another part of the show" (Kilpatrick 1999, 14–15). At the turn of the century, with his circus diminishing in popularity, Cody switched to moving pictures, starting his own studio and producing *The Indian Wars* (1914), a wildly successful propaganda piece directed by Theodore Wharton (Kilpatrick 1999, 20).

In describing the ambivalent relationship between Cody and the Sioux, Welch seems to be flirting with other Cowboy and Indian legends to be found in American film and fiction. The most universally known is Lone Ranger and his sidekick Tonto, played on radio from 1933 to 1955 and on television in the 1950s. This dynamic duo has more recently been reimagined by Spokane/Coeur d'Alene writer Sherman Alexie, whose book *The Lone Ranger and Tonto Fist Fight in Heaven* insinuates that there's a storm brewing between the honored cowboy and Indian. Actually, Tonto and the Lone Ranger never appear in Alexie's title story; these roles are assumed by two young men from Seattle, one of them a distrustful white 7–11 clerk and the other an Indian on a quest for a Creamsicle. The Indian in the story muses: "He knew this dark skin and long black hair of mine was dangerous" (Alexie 1993, 183).

Welch's French citizens also fear the dark skin and long black hair of their captive Indian. The French observe his enormous frame and find him grotesque. Charging Elk is caught between two identities; he desires to be assimilated, yet he is uncomfortable in his new surroundings and constantly remembers his former life on the Plains. In the conflict between Cody and Charging Elk lies the residual clash between the white man and the Red man, the Master and the Savage, underscored by the alienation of race and culture that marked the Plains Wars of the mid-nineteenth century. This confrontation persisted after the Indians were defeated, with the Sioux nation a ruined people.

In James Welch's depiction of the Wild West Show, Buffalo Bill and Charging Elk are estranged, so separated by matters of class that they never come into direct contact with each other. From a distance Charging Elk observes his white master standing aside from the other performers: He was at the "center of the crowd," dressed in the "fancy black clothes that the rich men of Paris wore in the evening" (57). In contrast, the Oglala Sioux, the stars of the Wild West, are dressed like savages, wearing only "breech cloths and moccasins and headdresses" (70). To Buffalo Bill, his star performer is one more piece of property. When his Redskin is lost, Cody picks up camp, making no effort to find him. The show must go on.

Welch's central character is an attractive and intelligent man with an adaptable character that allows him to assume many guises: horseman, circus performer, alien, worker, gentleman, lover, murderer, prisoner, husband. After he recovers from his near-death and subsequent escape from the hospital in Marseilles, Charging Elk wanders the streets until the authorities place him under the care of a kindhearted fish monger, Rene Soulas. As in his earlier novels, Welch shows great skill in his depiction of minor characters. The Soulas family had attended the Wild West Show when it played in Marseilles; Rene had "made savage whoops" when the *Peaux-Rouges* (Red Skins) defeated the Cavalry while his daughter, Chloe, had hidden her eyes at the sight of the "half-naked, flinty-eyed savages"

(112). Soulas, who operates a profitable fish stall in the port of Marseilles, gives the Indian a job selling fish. Charging Elk quickly adapts to his new services. Despite their cultural and racial differences, he discovers a home with the Soulas family and proves to be an excellent worker.

Although the initial characterization focuses on Charging Elk's role as abandoned alien, the emphasis on his self-identity becomes more pronounced as the novel progresses. As with all of his major characters, Welch reveals the "vivid internal world" of Charging Elk (Bloomstran 2002, 1). Welch plays his protagonist's innate stability against a shifting set of circumstances, many involving women, one of them detrimental to his personhood.

Unfortunately, the women characters in the novel are not fully realized. Rather, they serve as temptations or Deadly Sins, presenting moral distractions as Charging Elk pursues his quest for male identity. His ties with women characters are intricately connected to his personal/sexual development; but also, as in the case of Marie, they contribute to his downfall. Most of the women, beginning with Madeline Soulas, treat him with kindness. Although Chloe Soulas was at first shocked at seeing half-naked men at the Wild West Show, she soon befriends Charging Elk, teaching him French while her young female friends giggle in his presence. Charging Elk meets a woman at the fish market who arouses him, and he becomes infatuated with Sandrine, a saintly young woman whose goal is to convert him to Christianity. He looks with longing at, but does not touch, any of these women. Near the end of the novel, when his union goes on strike, Charging Elk apprehensively approaches the fish market, looking for work but primarily seeking the approval of Madeline Soulas. When she does not recognize him, he leaves, never to return (412). His final vision of Madeline Soulas parallels the failure of his personal dream: to be accepted in a country that is forever "strange" to him.

Charging Elk was introduced to sex by a wild Oglala woman whom he had encountered before coming to Europe. He thinks of her as a whore, a "crazy woman" who "opened her thighs for a bottle of holy water [whiskey]" (75). Marie, on the other hand, is a French prostitute who opens her thighs to keep her job. She is the first and only woman in the novel to use her sexuality to harm the hero. Of the long list of women characters with whom he forms ties, Marie is his most developed female. She is attracted to the big Indian, but she fears that if they were married he might return to America, "out of a job and a place," a phrase that she uses earlier as well to emphasize the economic limits on her life as a prostitute (273, 270).

In creating Marie, Welch was searching for historical accuracy, although the ruthless character Breteuil is almost a parody of the European homosexual philanderer. One critic describes him as "a fiendish gay chef with a yen for exotic-skinned lovers" (Miles 2000, 2). Marie was under pressure to cooperate with Breteuil, the odious man who has power over her. "She's afraid she'll lose her job. If she loses her job she'll be thrust into the street" ("Baltimore Interview"). Her motives, Welch argued, were economic. "She has to make a living. One of the things is that prostitutes were abused; they didn't have a very high standing. They were for the most part ignorant and illiterate. Their work span lasted a little while, and then they were done. They became char women or whatever" ("Baltimore Interview"). These remarks indicate that Welch had a cultural awareness of women within the historical setting he chose for his fifth novel. Although his sympathy for Marie seems genuine, Welch is again being ambivalent; Marie is not only an illiterate prostitute but also a manipulator. It is through her agency that the Sioux is drugged, duped, tried, and sent to prison.

Charging Elk's virginal wife Nathalie Gazier is clearly a foil to Marie. Nathalie Gazier is a pious teenager, the dutiful daughter of a farmer. She offers salvation to Charging Elk after the years spent in prison because of Marie's betrayal. Because she loves an Indian, Nathalie is forced to trade her dream of a Catholic wedding for a bleak civil ceremony. Like Rene Soulas, Nathalie's father is a kind and loving patriarch who tolerates Charging Elk until he learns that a romance has been festering under his roof. Although Vincent at first objects to the marriage between his daughter and an Indian, he finally gives them his blessing. Near the end of the novel Vincent experiences hard times and has to sell the farm.

Vincent Gazier seems to symbolize the father–son relationship of which Charging Elk is eternally deprived. Of the Sioux characters in the novel, they too seem like symbols or ideas rather than like real people. They represent beginnings and endings, highlighted figures who are by necessity excluded from the text.

## SETTING

The opening section or prologue to *The Heartsong of Charging Elk* is set in territory by now familiar to readers of Welch's works—on the banks of the Greasy Grass River in eastern Montana, where the united forces of the Sioux and the Cheyenne had defeated the Seventh Cavalry at the Battle of Little Bighorn on June 25, 1876. Welch had vividly described the Indian victory in *Killing Custer*. It is now nearly a year after the battle, 1877 by the settler calendar, during the Indian "Moon of the Shedding Ponies" (1). A boy and his people, worn and defeated, are being marched to the reservation.

Welch has opened the book so that the reader expects a novel set among the Sioux of South Dakota, as *Fools Crow* (1986) had been set among the Blackfeet of Montana. But as *Charging Elk* formally begins, there is an extraordinary shift in setting, from the bright hills above the Little Bighorn to an unknown location in the darkness. Unlike his other novels, unlike most works written by Native American authors, *The Heartsong of Charging Elk* is set in Europe. The familiar scents of plains and prairie—the smells of pheasants, alfalfa, and the corral that Welch had eulogized in our Montana interview—have vanished, replaced by the smells of fish, the sea, chestnuts, and livestock (39–40).

Most of *The Heartsong of Charging Elk* is set in the southern French town of Marseilles. Welch said, "I really wanted to make this a novel of the reality of the turn of the century in a port city as I could imagine it" ("Baltimore Interview"). For Charging Elk, lost in France, the setting is forbidding and out of context, not something he can easily adjust to, any more than he was able to adjust to life on the reservation. He is exposed to a place where there is typhoid, stench, and prostitution, but a place "thick with atmosphere and rich in ambience" (Knickerbocker 2000, 16). Marseilles is also a city of many wonders, with its cafes and carriages, its women carrying baskets of produce on their heads (40). Charging Elk learns to love his environment, to become part of it, until the fateful day when he is tried and found guilty for the murder of Breteuil.

The most oppressive setting is the jail. Sentenced to life imprisonment, Charging Elk is sent to La Tombe in southwestern France. Like the dank Bastille in Charles Dickens's *The Tale of Two Cities*, La Tombe has underground cells and stone walls "three meters thick" (344). Prisoners sequestered there "would never see the gardens or the village again" (345). One inmate recognizes Charging Elk as a member of Buffalo Bill's troupe. They are cellmates for three years, until the warden assigns his model prisoner to tend the garden of the institution. At that point the setting shifts from the darkness inside the prison to the natural light of the landscape, with distant houses whose roofs look like "circus tents," with hills more colorful and lush than those in Paha Sapa (355). Charging Elk works there without complaining until he is suddenly released.

Again Charging Elk is forced to adjust to a new environment, this time to an orchard. His hard labor, both in the prison garden and in the orchard, echoes the conclusion of *Candide*, as discussed in the next section. Even more so, it represents a revitalization of spirit and a rememory of the Black Hills. Although the orchard setting is far more domesticated than the wilderness of South Dakota, it nonetheless helps him to unearth the man he left behind.

## THEMATIC ISSUES

One reviewer rightly argues that the central theme of *The Heartsong of Charging Elk* is "abandonment" (Archuleta 2001, 185). Charging Elk is abandoned by the Oglala Sioux who perform for Buffalo Bill in Marseilles, and then by Buffalo Bill himself, his only ticket home. He lies abandoned in a hospital in Southern France, then escapes to the streets, emerging into a lonely world of isolation and unhealth where he is abandoned by a society that refuses to look past the largeness of his frame or the darkness of his skin. When he falls in love with Marie, she abandons him for fear that he will desert her.

At the heart of the theme of abandonment Welch resurrects the historical figure of Buffalo Bill. The Indian participation in the Buffalo Bill Show and the marketing of Indian warriors is one of the most unsettling themes in *The Heartsong of Charging Elk*. The theme of abandonment is reversed at the end of the novel. Charging Elk, in rejecting the pleas of his countrymen, sacrifices his dream of returning to his homeland, replacing it with the reality of his prudent marriage and his forthcoming child.

Another major theme relates to contrast between civilization and "savagery," the former represented by the city and the white man and the latter by the wilderness and by the Indian (Fees 1990, 146). Animals such as the buffalo and the pony, so integral to the wilderness of the Western Plains, are now, like the Indians, mere circus performers. Charging Elk is proud to dress in his elegant costume and ride a grand horse, although he "knew that it was all fake" (52). Unlike his Blackfeet counterparts who roamed the hills of Montana in *Fools Crow*, Charging Elk abandons his native surroundings in the South Dakota Black Hills and chooses to join the show, to become part of what, according to Welch, was essentially an "urban affair." Because the nighttime was taken up in travel, the performers often had no idea of the countryside. "The show played seven months in Paris, so they became used to Paris as a city" ("Baltimore Interview").

Ironically, the big Indian's achievement at survival in the wilderness is what Buffalo Bill had found so appealing. After leaving the Sacred Hills and surviving the city of Marseilles, Charging Elk forever carries the holy land of the Sioux in his memories. He eventually learns to adapt his wilderness environment into a new form of nature, exchanging the wild forests for disciplined rows of fruit trees.

Charging Elk's salvation through agriculture may remind the reader of Voltaire's *Candide* (1789), one of France's most celebrated pieces of literature. At the end of the short novel Candide is in a garden with a few friends, all of them survivors. Pangloss, the romantic, speculates about what a better life it might have been. "Excellently observed," answered Candide; "but we must cultivate our gardens" (Voltaire [1789] 1999, Chapter 30, ll. 158–59).

The rationalist conclusion of *Candide* is a fitting answer to the question of how geography affects theme in *The Heartsong of Charging Elk*: Which is better—to cultivate one's orchard or always to desire to return to a land of broken dreams? The Paradise continues when Charging Elk is released to the farm of Vincent Gazier, but like most earthly Paradises, it is short-lived.

The animals that had so great a thematic role in Welch's first three novels become, like Sitting Bull and Red Cloud, peripheral figures, performers in Cody's sideshow. In removing the Indians, the horses, and the buffalo from the western Plains to eastern and European cities, "Buffalo" Bill mimicked the cultural upheaval of the half century following the Civil War, turning wilderness into civilization and transforming the harsh experience of Indian captivity into an entertainment. The "deeper themes" of the novel are "wed to this contrapuntal movement between Charging Elk's vivid recollections of Native life on the American plains and his contrasting impressions of life in a bustling and gritty European port" (Tack 2000, 56).


## STYLE AND LITERARY DEVICES

The *bildungsroman* is a literary work that traces "the development of a young person, usually from adolescence to maturity" (Harmon and Holman 2000, 59). In *Fools Crow* the reader follows White Man's Dog from his development as a boy of 18 winters to his maturity as a prophet and keeper of the medicine. In *The Heartsong of Charging Elk*, in contrast, the protagonist's tribal development is disrupted by the reservation system. In retreating to the Black Hills, Charging Elk reaches his maturity in the wilds, without the rituals of the Sioux people that would have provided him with guidance and direction. Consequently there are huge gaps in his development. He grows up like an animal or a wild child, then is transplanted to a strange culture where the French find his Oglala language to be indecipherable.

As in *Fools Crow* before it, so in his fifth novel Welch devotes much of his stylistic attention to the act of translating Charging Elk's language and cultural foundations into an intelligible experience for Euro-American readers. To achieve this goal Welch has "devised a strong plain style for Charging Elk that suggests the rhythms and concepts of the Lakota language" (Frase 2002, 20). Almost every reviewer has praised the strength of the prose. Johnathan Miles writes that "the novel moves with sensual grace—slow but never sluggish, and always seeming, with its plain measured cadences, to be building toward something, to be growing inside itself" (Miles 2000, 2). Brad Knickerbocker commends Welch's "clear, lucid prose suitable to the restraint of his hero" (Knickerbocker 2000, 16). The novel is punctuated with memories of Charging Elk's past on the Plains, memories that "generate the novel's most powerful prose" (White 2001, 1).

Most discussions of the novel, though they address Welch's plot, style, and character development, tend to avoid any direct reference to his erotic style, specifically to the unrestrained scene in which Charging Elk stabs his tormentor. Awakening from a drugged sleep, he sees a man's mouth "sliding up and down on the smooth shaft of his cock" (276). I asked Welch if he was concerned that the softly pornographic passage might make him liable to censorship or make teachers unwilling to order the novel for their literature students. He told me that schools in Montana had tried to ban *Fools Crow* because of the episode in which Yellow Kidney fornicates with a Crow woman who is dying of smallpox. "People were shocked, but the School Board voted nine to nothing to keep it. Now in *The Heartsong of Charging Elk* I guess the sex is a little more shocking because it's Europeanized. It's about prostitutes and the abuse of prostitutes by these men who get drunk and want to beat them up" ("Baltimore Interview").

We discussed the homosexuality of the passage in question, the outrageous act that in Sioux tradition would warrant revenge. "I think it's something that even sophisticated readers, contemporary readers, would be shocked by," Welch remarked with a trickster's gleam in his eyes. "I felt really great about that" ("Baltimore Interview").

As in all of his novels, Welch contrasts Native American tradition and its European counterparts. In *The Heartsong of Charging Elk*, though, the stylistic and thematic formulas of the Native American vision quest become subordinated to the European novel of romance. Charging Elk's untamed freedom in the post-reservation wilderness is replaced by the albeit pleasant constrictions of marriage and family, in a "weird little sort-

of-happily-ever-after ending" which does disservice to the political con-
tent and to the narrative form (Burghart 2000, 2).

With the publication of *The Heartsong of Charging Elk* in 2000, James
Welch established his reputation as a leader in contemporary fiction. His
five novels and his work in poetry, nonfiction, and film scripting distinguish him as a participant in what has been called the Indian cultural
Renaissance. In Baltimore I asked Welch if he had witnessed a cultural
renewal in Native American writing. He said, "Sure, sure. It's been going
on for 30 years. Ever since Momaday's *House Made of Dawn*. At first it
started out very small. I think there was Momaday, me, Leslie Silko, Simon
Ortiz, Joy Harjo—people like that were there kind of at the beginning.
Then [Adrian] Louis came along pretty soon, so it's been growing, out-
ward, so you get people like Sherman Alexie, who's the new star. He's
really a great guy. I think he takes Indian literature in a slightly different
direction."

In an interview with Cindy Heidemann Welch expressed a similar faith
in an Indian Renaissance, adding less established literary figures to his
list: "Claire Davis (*Winter Range*), Brady Udall (*Letting Loose the Hounds*),
Diane Smith (*Letters from Yellowstone*), to name just a few. Our literature is
in great shape" ("Author Interview" 2002, 3).

A reaffirmation of cultural ancestry dominates contemporary Indian
literature; an awareness of historical fact also involves the act of self-
discovery through tribal identification and a knowledge of the past. In his
written works James Phillip Welch has demonstrated, as much as any
other Indian novelist, "a process of recovery, a conscious act of reclaiming
knowledge of a tribal self" (Teuton 2001, 626).

Native writers are, each of them, successors to their ancestors. Like his
great-grandmother, Red Paint Woman, James Welch, though deceased, is
nonetheless a survivor of the Marias River massacre of 1870. In retelling
the story of Charging Elk, a Sioux, he is also retelling the story of Red
Paint Woman and of the vanishing American—from a different cultural
perspective but with an awareness of how the Seventh Cavalry and the
reservation system are still destroying Indians more than a century and a
half later.

## ALTERNATIVE READING: A FEMINIST APPROACH

Feminism is a system of thought that focuses on women's issues. It
investigates the role of women at home, at work, and in all areas that
affect women's lives, such as politics, medicine, and the media. A basic

feminist belief is that women live in a system dominated by men. Women who challenge this system are feminists, whether they identify with the term or not.

Feminist criticism examines literature in an effort to show the extent to which writers, both women and men, have demonstrated an awareness of women characters and of those social conditions affecting women. It is not a single theory but a multiple application of various approaches to literature; it is, nonetheless, always concerned with issues of gender.

During the early 1970s, when Welch was writing *Winter in the Blood*, there was an upsurge of feminist politics, a New Women's Movement that was indebted, as was the American Indian Movement, to the Civil Rights Movement of the 1960s, with its grassroots appeal and its strategies for social change (Lupton 1998, 70–71). Native American women, placed on reservations and denied educational opportunities, were in 1970 the lowest paid workers in America, earning only $1,700 annually (Olson and Wilson 1986, 186). Although the actual statistics have changed in the twenty-first century, the distribution of capital for most Indian women has not improved. Damaged by low incomes and racial stereotyping, Indian women have tended to separate themselves from national groups such as the National Association for the Advancement of Colored People (NAACP), the National Organization for Women (NOW), and other non-Indian organizations, choosing Indian women's coalitions in their efforts to change working and living conditions.

Chief Mark Gould told me that the NAACP, initially founded to help all people of color, has neglected the economic and social conditions of Native Americans, despite comparable problems (Lupton 2002). According to one source, Indian women reject the idea of women's liberation, claiming that "they cannot afford the luxury of feminist goals because they must devote their energies to keeping families intact, getting jobs, and fighting the political battles of their people" (Bataille and Sands [1984] 1987, 129).

Although it is customary for a feminist critic to address women's writing, it is possible to look at *The Heartsong of Charging Elk* from a feminist perspective. Steven Lynn argues that even if a novel does not emphasize women characters, "the absence of women or their concerns may be quite significant" (Lynn 1998, 180). In Welch's earlier novels women characters are important mainly as they relate to men. Teresa, Rhea, Red Paint, Patti Ann Harwood, and other women affect the plot of each novel as mothers, wives, and mistresses. Unlike Paula Gunn Allen or Leslie Marmon Silko or Linda Hogan, Welch does not focus on the welfare of Indian women or of his Indian women characters.

There are exceptions to this general pattern. Welch praises Mildred Walker's *Winter Wheat* for its emphasis on women's issues: "It is a story about growing up, becoming a woman, mentally, emotionally, and spiritually, within the space of a year and a half" (Introduction, *Winter Wheat* 1992). *Fools Crow* clearly indicates that Welch had researched Blackfeet history and has represented women's roles as contributing members of the economy. According to Barbara Cook, women provide "strength and centrality" in Welch's contemporary novels as well (Cook 2000, 441). But he seems to subordinate even his strong women characters—for example, Lena Old Horn, the counselor in *The Indian Lawyer*—to a nonessential position.

When asked if he had a feminist perspective, Welch expressed his attitude in an unequivocal way: "Yes, well, I'm as feminist as it's necessary to be in terms of my narratives" ("Baltimore Interview"). He has doubtlessly put his art over politics.

In *The Heartsong of Charging Elk* women play an even lesser role than they do in the earlier novels, tending to meet the hero's needs as objects of his desire. A feminist critic would find Charging Elk's adoration of Marie to be problematic, similar to the Indian lawyer's attitude toward Patti Ann, who initially was involved in a conspiracy to blackmail him. In both cases Indian men are blindly infatuated with white women, a psycho-sexual bonding with precedents in literature, film, and other narrative forms. Welch explains his character's desires as the normal responses of a spirited young man: "He's a young man. He's lonely. What could he want more than to have an actual partner he can love? That's the ideal" ("Baltimore Interview"). Yet except for his young wife, women are not actual partners but means to an end.

With two single exceptions, the women who tempt him are French. The first anomaly is the wild Oglala woman who trades sex for whiskey. The second is a more complex figure, a Sioux named Sarah whom he encounters at the end of the novel, a woman with "long braids" and smooth skin "the color of pecans" (431). If there is an erotic attraction, it is only for a flicker: "Charging Elk looked away from Sarah" (434).

The issue of miscegenation is a controversial matter in Native American and African American literature. It has peculiar implications in *The Heartsong of Charging Elk*, since with the women of the Oglala tribe lost to him, European women are the only options, just as French is the only option for oral communication. The Sioux woman, Sarah, though attractive, is simply too late because of Charging Elk's commitment to his pregnant wife, Nathalie, his heart of hearts. To return to America, either to uproot Nathalie from her culture—or perhaps, even, to seek an additional mate among his people—is therefore a prerogative that he emphatically rejects.

In his fifth novel James Welch settles any unresolved sexual conflict by restricting his ardent male hero to the confines of a European nuclear family, with its model of mother, father, and child-to-be. This grouping is consistent with the culture Charging Elk has adopted during his long estrangement from the Lakota people. Although his tribe resides in his memory throughout the novel, when they appear in the flesh Charging Elk is jolted into the present. Knowing that the circle is broken, he wends his way by moonlight, past the empty stalls, past the bleachers that "looked like distant mountains" (438), toward his new family. If James Welch had intended to return his Indian to the distant hills of America, there is no evidence of that plan in the novel's poignant ending.

# Bibliography

**WORKS BY JAMES WELCH**

## Fiction

*The Death of Jim Loney*. New York: Harper, 1979.
*Fools Crow*. New York: Penguin, 1986.
*The Heartsong of Charging Elk*. New York: Doubleday, 2000.
*The Indian Lawyer*. New York: Penguin, 1991.
"The Loose Screw." From *Marseilles Gracen* (early draft of *The Heartsong of Charging Elk*). *Weber Studies* 12:3 (Fall, 1995) <http://weberstudies.weber.edu/archive/Vol%2012.3/12.3Welch.htm>.
*Winter in the Blood*. New York: Harper, 1974.

## Nonfiction

*Killing Custer*. With Paul Stekler. New York: Penguin, 1994.

## Poetry (excluding anthologized poems)

*Riding the Earth Boy 40*. 1971. Pittsburgh: Carnegie Mellon University Press, 1997.

## Prefaces, Editing, and Drafts

Ed., with Lois Welch, and Ripley S. Hugo. *The Real West Marginal Way: A Poet's Autobiography*. By Richard Hugo. New York: W. W. Norton, 1986.

Guest Editor. "Tribes." *Ploughshares* 20.1 (Spring 1994): 193–97.

Foreword. *The Reservation Blackfeet, 1882–1945: A Photographic History of Cultural Survival*. By William E. Farr. Seattle: University of Washington Press, 1984. vii–viii.

Introduction. *Third Catalog of Native American Literature*. Hadley, MA: Ken Lopez Bookseller, 1997. 19 June 2002 <http://www.lopezbooks.com/articles/welch/html>.

Introduction. *Winter Wheat*. By Mildred Walker. Lincoln: University of Nebraska Press, 1992.

## Descriptive Texts and Illustrations

Haselstrom, Linda, and James Welch. *Bison: Monarch of the Plains*. Photographs by David Fitzgerald. Portland, OR: Graphic Arts Center Publishing Co., 1998.

Hugo, Richard. *Death and the Good Life*. James Welch, illustrator. New York: St. Martin's Press, 1982. Moscow, ID: University of Idaho Press, 2002.

Limerick, Patricia Nelson, and James Welch. *Sweet Medicine: Sites of Indian Massacres, Battlefields, and Treaties*. Photographs by Drew Brooks. Albuquerque: University of New Mexico Press, 1995.

## BIOGRAPHICAL SOURCES

Lee, Don. "About James Welch." *Ploughshares* 20 (1994):193–99.

"Montana Author James Welch Dies." *The Salt Lake City Tribune* 8 Aug. 2003 <http://www.sltrib.com/2003/Aug/08072003/thursday/81876.asp>.

Saxon, Wolfgang. "James Welch, 62, an Indian Who Wrote about the Plains, Dies." *New York Times* 10 Aug. 2003 <wysiwyg://http://www.nytimes.com/2003/08/09/arts/09WELC.html>.

*Yale Bulletin and Calendar* 29:8 (October 2000): 1–2.

## Selected Interviews

Welch, James. "Wylie Tales: An interview with James Welch." With William Bevis. *Weber Studies* 12:3 (Fall 1995): 1–14 <http://weberstudies.weber.edu/archive/archive/%20B%20Vol.%2011.6/5/02>.

———. "Author Interview." With Cindy Heidemann. 9 May 2002 <http://www.pnba.org/welch.htm>.

———. "Baltimore Interview." With Mary Jane Lupton. 17 November 2001.

———. "Montana Interview." With Mary Jane Lupton. 10 July 2002.

———. "Interview with Ron McFarland." *James Welch*. Ed. R. McFarland. Lewiston, ID: Confluence Press, 1986.

## Audio and Film Interviews

*American Audio Prose Library: An Interview with James Welch.* With Kay Bonetti. April 1985. Columbia, MO: Western Historical Manuscript Collection.
*Native American Novelists Series: James Welch Humanities.* Films for the Humanities and Sciences. 1999.

## Critical Views of the Novels

Chester, Blanca Schorcht. "Storied Voices in Native American Texts: Harry Robinson, Thomas King, James Welch, and Leslie Marmon Silko." *Dissertation Abstracts International* 61.5 (Nov. 2000): 1826.
McFarland, Ron, ed. *James Welch.* Lewiston, ID: Confluence Press, 1986.
———. *Understanding James Welch.* Columbia, SC: University of South Carolina Press, 2000.
Sands, Kathleen Mullen. "Closing the Distance: Critic, Reader and the Works of James Welch." *MELUS* 14.2 (Summer 1987): 73–85.
Vizenor, Gerald, ed. *Narrative Chance: Postmodern Discourses on Native American Literature.* Albuquerque: University of New Mexico Press, 1989.

## CRITICISM AND REVIEWS OF INDIVIDUAL NOVELS AND NONFICTION

### *Winter in the Blood*

Ballard, Charles G. "The Theme of the Helping in *Winter in the Blood.*" *MELUS* 17.1 (1991–1992): 3–20.
Barnett, Louise K. "Alienation and Ritual in *Winter in the Blood.*" Beidler 122–30.
Barry, Nora Baker. "*Winter in the Blood* as Elegy." Beidler 149–58.
Beidler, Peter G., ed. Spec. Symposium Issue on *Winter in the Blood. American Indian Quarterly* 4 (May 1978).
Beidler, Peter G., and A. LaVonne Ruoff, eds. "A Discussion of *Winter in the Blood.*" Beidler 159–68.
Davis, Jack. "Restoration of Indian Identity in *Winter in the Blood.*" *James Welch.* Ed. Ron McFarland. Lewiston, ID: Confluence Press, 1986. 29–44.
Eisenstein, Paul. "Finding Lost Generations: Recovering Omitted History in *Winter in the Blood.*" *MELUS* 19.3 (Fall 1994): 3–18.
Gish, Robert. "Mystery and Mock Intrigue in James Welch's *Winter in the Blood.*" *James Welch.* Ed. Ron McFarland. Lewiston, ID: Confluence Press, 1986. 45–58.
Horton, Andrew. "The Bitter Humor of *Winter in the Blood.*" Beidler 131–40.
Kunz, Don. "Lost in the Distance of Winter: James Welch's *Winter in the Blood.*" *Critique* 20 (1978): 93–99.
Lincoln, Kenneth. "Back-Tracking James Welch." *MELUS* 6.1 (1979): 23–40.

Norden, Christopher. "Ecological Restoration as Post-Colonial Ritual of Community in Three Native American Novels." *Studies in American Indian Literatures* 6.4 (Winter 1994): 94–106.

Ruffino, K. "An Interesting Look at American Indian Lifestyles." Customer Reviews: *Winter in the Blood* (Contemporary America) 11 Nov. 2001 <http://www.amazon.com/exec/obidos/tg/stor/...iews/ref=pm_dp_ln_b_7/103-2295296-5584669>.

Ruoff, A. LaVonne. "Alienation and the Female Principle in *Winter in the Blood*." Beidler 107–21.

———. "History in *Winter in the Blood*: Backgrounds and Bibliography." Beidler 169–72.

———. "The Influence of Elio Vittorini's *In Sicily* on James Welch's *Winter in the Blood*." *Native American Literatures: Forum* (Pisa) 1 (1989): 151–157.

Sands, Kathleen M. "Alienation and Broken Narrative in *Winter in the Blood*." Beidler 97–106.

Tatum, Stephen. "'Distance,' Desire, and the Ideological Matrix of *Winter in the Blood*." *Arizona Quarterly* 46.2 (1990): 73–100.

Teuton, Sean. "Placing the Ancestors: Postmodernism, 'Realism,' and American Indian Identity in James Welch's *Winter in the Blood*." *American Indian Quarterly* 25.4 (Fall 2001): 626–50.

Thackeray, William W. "Animal Allies and Transformations in *Winter in the Blood*." *MELUS* 12 (Spring 1985): 37–64.

Velie, Alan R. "*Winter in the Blood* as Comic Novel." Beidler 141–49.

## *The Death of Jim Loney*

Antell, Judith A. "Momaday, Welch, and Silko: Expressing the Female Principle Through Male Alienation." *American Indian Quarterly* (Summer 1988): 213–20.

In-the-Woods, Patricia Riley. "*The Death of Jim Loney*: A Ritual of Re-Creation." *Fiction International* 20 (1991): 164–71.

Kiely, Robert. Rev. of *The Death of Jim Loney*. *New York Times Book Review* 4 Nov. 1979: 14.

Klein, C. M. Rev. of *The Death of Jim Loney*. *Library Journal* 1.104 (Sept. 1979): 1722.

Logan, William. Rev. of *The Death of Jim Loney*. *Saturday Review of Books* 10 Nov. 1979: 54.

Sands, Kathleen. "The Death of Jim Loney: Indian or Not." *James Welch*. Ed. Ron McFarland. Lexington, ID: Confluence Press, 1986. 127–33.

Thackeray, William W. "The Dance of Jim Loney." *James Welch*. Ed. Ron McFarland. Lexington, ID: Confluence Press, 1986. 135–37.

Westrum, Dexter. "Transcendental Survival: The Way the Bird Works in *The Death of Jim Loney*." *James Welch*. Ed. Ron McFarland. Lexington, ID: Confluence Press, 1986. 139–45.

## Fools Crow

Bak, Hans. "The Art of Hybridization—James Welch's *Fools Crow.*" *American Studies in Scandinavia* 27.1 (1995): 33–47.

Ballard, Charles G. "The Question of Survival in *Fools Crow.*" *North Dakota Quarterly* 59.4 (1991): 251–59.

Barry, Nora. "'A Myth to Be Alive': James Welch's *Fools Crow.*" *MELUS* 17.1 (Spring 1991–1992): 3–20.

Berner, Robert L. Rev. of *Fools Crow. World Lit Today* 61 (Spring 1987): 333.

Cook, Barbara. "A Tapestry of History and Reimagination: Women's Place in James Welch's *Fools Crow.*" *American Indian Quarterly* 24:3 (2000): 441–53.

King, T. Rev. of *Fools Crow. Choice* 24 (Apr. 1987): 1223.

Shanley, Kathryn W. "The Cinematic Eye in James Welch's *Fools Crow.*" *Ethnic Voices II.* Ed. Claudine Reynaud. 1996. 131–38.

Wild, Peter. Rev. of *Fools Crow. New York Times Book Review* 2 Nov. 1986: 14.

## The Indian Lawyer

Donahue, Peter. "New Warriors, New Legends: Basketball in Three Native American Works of Fiction." *American Indian Culture and Research Journal* 21.2 (1997): 43–60.

Hoagland, Edward. Rev. of *The Indian Lawyer. New York Times Book Review* 25 Nov. 1990: 7.

Larson, Sidner J. "The Outsider in James Welch's *The Indian Lawyer.*" *American Indian Quarterly* 18 (Fall 1994): 495–506.

———. Rev. of *The Indian Lawyer. Studies in American Indian Literature* 2.3 (Fall 1991): 65–66.

Parins, J. W. Rev. of *The Indian Lawyer. Choice* 28 (Mar. 1991): 1139.

Seals, David. Rev. of *The Indian Lawyer. Nation* 26 Nov. 1990: 648.

## Killing Custer

Carr, Helen. Rev. of *Killing Custer. New Statesman* 8 (31 Mar. 1995): 39.

Freeman, Jay. Rev. of *Killing Custer. Booklist* 91 (1 Nov. 1994): 477.

White, Richard. Rev. of *Killing Custer. New York Times Book Review,* 30 Apr. 1995: 31.

## The Heartsong of Charging Elk

Archuleta, Elizabeth. Rev. of *The Heartsong of Charging Elk. World Literature Today* 75.1 (Winter 2001): 185.

Bloomstran, Shannon. Rev. of *The Heartsong of Charging Elk* 1 Mar. 2002 <http://mostlyfiction.com/west/welch.htm>.

Bogenschutz, Debbie. Rev. of *The Heartsong of Charging Elk*. *Library Journal* 125.8 (May 2000): 155.

Burghart, D. Brian. Rev. of *The Heartsong of Charging Elk*. *Arts and Culture* 11 Nov. 2000: 1–3 <http://www.newsreview.com/issues/sacto/2000-11-30/book.asp>.

DeSpain, Lori. Rev. of *The Heartsong of Charging Elk*. *School Library Journal* 47.2 (Feb. 2001): 144.

Frase, Brigette. "Off the Rez." Rev. of *The Heartsong of Charging Elk*. *New York Times Book Review* 1 Sept. 2002: 20.

Knickerbocker, Brad. Rev. of *The Heartsong of Charging Elk*. *Christian Science Monitor* 21 Sept. 2000: 16.

Methot, Suzanne. Rev. of *The Heartsong of Charging Elk*. *Windspeaker* 18.6 (Oct. 2000): 21.

Miles, Jonathan. Rev. of *The Heartsong of Charging Elk*. *Salon.com* 15 Aug. 2000: 1–2 <Wysiwyg://67//http://www.salon.com/books/review/2000/08/15/Welch>.

Pearl, Nancy, and Jennifer Young. "Native Voices, Old and New." *Library Journal* 127.14 (1 Sept. 2002): 244.

Peck, David. Rev. of *The Heartsong of Charging Elk*. *Magill Book Reviews* 1 May 2001: Record 2.

Tack, Alan. Rev. of *The Heartsong of Charging Elk*. *Native Peoples* 13 (Sept./Oct. 2000): 6.

White, Emily. Rev. of *The Heartsong of Charging Elk*. *amazon.com* 11 Oct. 2001: 1–6 <http://www.amazon.com/exec/obidos/tg/stor....ieews/ref=pm_dp_ln_b_6/103-2295296-5584669>.

## OTHER SECONDARY SOURCES

### Blackfeet and Other Native American Traditions

Alexie, Sherman. *The Lone Ranger and Tonto Fist Fight in Heaven*. New York: HarperPerennial, 1993.

Allen, Paula Gunn. "Globalization and Indigenous View." Paper presented at All Women of Red Nations: Weaving Connections Conference. Southern Connecticut State University, New Haven. 12 Oct. 2001.

———. *The Sacred Hoop: Recovering the Feminine in American Indian Traditions*. Boston: Beacon Press, 1986.

Bataille, Gretchen M., and Kathleen Mullen Sands. *American Indian Women*. 1984. Lincoln: University of Nebraska Press, 1987.

Beinart, Peter. "Lost Tribes." *Lingua Franca* (May/June 1999): 33–41.

Benedict, Jeff. *Without Reservation*. New York: HarperCollins, 2000.

Bevis, William. "Native American Novels: Homing In." *Critical Perspectives on Na-*

*tive American Fiction*. Ed. Richard F. Fleck. Washington, DC: Three Conti-
    nents Press, 1993. 15–45.

"The Blackfoot Indians." *Britannica Online*. 6 June 2002 <http://uts.cc.utexas.edu/
    awk/blackfoot.html>.

Brokaw, Chet. "Oglala Sioux Struggle with Future of Tribal Government." *The
    Telegraph Online* 22 May 2000: 1.

Brown, Dee. *Bury My Heart at Wounded Knee: An Indian History of the American
    West*. 1970. New York: Henry Holt and Company, Owl Book Edition, 1991.

Brown, Joseph Epes. *Animals of the Soul*. 1992. Rev. ed. Rockport, MA: Element
    Books, 1997.

Bruchac, James, and Joseph Bruchac. *Native American Games and Stories*. Golden,
    CO: Fulcrum Publishers, 2000.

Colton, Larry. *Counting Coup*. New York: Warner Books, 2001.

Day, Grove A. *The Sky Clears: Poetry of the American Indians*. 1951. Lincoln: Uni-
    versity of Nebraska Press, 1964.

Deloria, Vine. *Custer Died for Your Sins: An Indian Manifesto*. New York: Macmillan,
    1969.

Donovan, Kathleen M. *Feminist Readings of Native American Literature*. Tucson: Uni-
    versity of Arizona Press, 1998.

Earling, Debra Magpie. *Perma Red*. New York: Bantam Blue Hen, 2003. In 2003
    Bantam catalog. Description by James Welch.

Erdoes, Richard, and Alfonson Ortiz. *American Indian Trickster Tales*. New York:
    Penguin, 1999.

Erdrich, Louise. *Love Medicine*. New York: Bantam Books, 1984.

Ewers, John Canfield. *The Emergence of the Plains Indian as the Symbol of the North
    American Indian*. Washington, DC: Library of Congress, 1965.

Farr, William E. *The Reservation Blackfeet, 1882–1945: A Photographic History of Cul-
    tural Survival*. Seattle: University of Washington Press, 1984.

Fees, Paul. "In Defense of Buffalo Bill: A Look at Cody in and of his Time." *Myth
    of the West*. Seattle: Henry Art Gallery; New York: Rizzoli, 1990. 141–49.

Feldmann, Susan, ed. *The Storytelling Stone: Traditional Native American Myths and
    Tales*. New York: Dell, 1965.

Forbes, Jack D. *Africans and Native Americans*. 2nd ed. Urbana: University of Illinois
    Press, 1993.

Giago, Tim. "Searching for Happy Town: Remembering SuAnne." *The Lakota Na-
    tion Journal* 7–13 Feb. 2000: 1–3.

Gibson, Daniel. "Native Scientists Taking Off." *Native Peoples* 1 (Nov./Dec. 2002):
    26–31.

Gildart, Bert. "History Revisited at the Infamous Little Bighorn." *Native Peoples*
    14:8 (July/August 2001): 60–63.

Grinnell, George Bird. *Blackfeet Indian Stories*. 1913. New York: Charles Scribner's
    Sons, 1926. Facsim. ed. Bedford, CT: Applewood Books, 1993.

———. *Blackfoot Lodge Tales*. 1892. Lincoln: University of Nebraska Press, 1962.

Habets, Jerry. *Glacier Guide*. 19 May 2002: 4–5.

Hill, Liz. "Gambling Traditions Run Deep in Native America." *Native Peoples* 16:3 (Mar/Apr 2003): 46–47.

Horne, Dee. *Contemporary American Indian Writing*. New York: Peter Lang Publishing, 1999.

———. "How Dogs Came to the Indians." 12 June 1999 <wiswyg:36/http:// geocities.com/RainForest/5292/dog.htm>.

Kent, Jim. "Pigs Estimated to Generate $5 Million a Year." *The New Lakota Times* 11–17 Oct. 1999: 1–a2.

King, Thomas. *Medicine River*. 1989. New York: Penguin Putnam, 1991.

Kittredge, William, and Annick Smith, eds. *The Last Best Place: A Montana Anthology*. Seattle: University of Washington Press, 1990.

Klein, Janice. Dir. "Learning to Play: Playing to Learn." Special Exhibit. Mitchell Museum of the American Indian. Kendall College, Evanston, IL. Phone interview with Mary Jane Lupton. 31 Oct. 2002.

Lang, Kristine A. "Gros Ventre." 25 June 2002 <http://www.anthro.mankato. msus.edu/cultural/northamerica/gros_ventre.html>.

Little Rock [Timothy Reed]. "The American Indian in the White Man's Prisons: A Story of Genocide." *Humanity & Society* 1989. 2 Apr. 2003 <http://www. jpp.org/fulltext-v2/jppv2n1-f.html>.

Louis, Adrian C. *Skins*. New York: Crown Publishing Group, 1995.

Lupton, Mary Jane. "Interview with Len'ape Indians." Cape May, NJ. 5 Sept. 2002.

Mackie, Mary M. "Status, Mixedbloods, and Community in Thomas King's *Medicine River*." *Journal of American Studies in Turkey* 8 (1998): 65–71. 6 June 2002 <http://www.bilkent.edu.tr/~jast/Number8/Mackie.html>.

Marks, Paula Mitchell. *In a Barren Land: American Indian Dispossession and Survival*. New York: William Morrow, 1998.

McClintock, Walter. *The Old North Trail: Life, Legends and Religion of the Blackfeet Indians*. 1968. Lincoln: University of Nebraska Press, 1999.

Momaday, N. Scott. *House Made of Dawn*. 1934. New York: Harper, 1966. Madison, WI: TurtleBack Books, 1999.

———. "And We Have Only Begun to Define Our Destiny." *Native Peoples* 15: 5 (Jul./Aug. 2002): 12–13.

Neihardt, John G., ed. *Black Elk Speaks*. 1932. Lincoln: University of Nebraska Press, 1998.

Nelson, Robert M. *Place and Vision*. New York: Peter Lang Publishing, 1993.

Nichols, K. R. "Native American Trickster Tales." 3 Dec. 2002 <http://www.pitt state.edu/engl/nichols/coyote.html>.

Nijhuis, Michelle. "Tribal Immersion School Rescue Language and Culture." *The Christian Science Monitor* 11 June 2002: 11+.

Olson, James S., and Raymond Wilson. *Native Americans in the Twentieth Century*. Urbana: University of Illinois Press, 1986.

Owens, Louis. *Other Destinies*. 1992. Norman: University of Oklahoma Press, 1994.

Oxendine, Joseph B. *American Indian Sports Heritage*. Champaign, IL: Human Ki-
    netics Books, 1988.

Peltier, Leonard. *Prison Writings: My Life Is My Sun Dance*. 1999. New York: St.
    Martin's Griffin, 2000.

Pritzker, Barry M. *A Native American Encyclopedia*. New York: Oxford University
    Press, 2000.

Roberts, Chris. *Powwow Country: People of the Circle*. Missoula, MT: Meadowlark
    Publishing Company, 1998.

Ross, Allen C. *Mitakuye Oyasin: "We All Are Related."* Centennial ed. Fort Yates,
    ND: Bear, 1989.

Sams, Jamie, and David Carson. *Medicine Cards: The Discovery of Power through the
    Way of Animals*. 2 vols. Illustrated by Angela C. Werneke. Santa Fe, NM:
    Bear and Company, 1988.

Sanchez, Jennifer W. "Jailed U.S. Indians Lack Rituals Access, Ally Says." 2 Apr.
    2003 <http://mytwobeadsworth.com/JailedNA11403.html>.

Schultz, James Willard. *My Life as an Indian*. 1907. Lewiston, ID: Confluence Press,
    1983.

Seals, David. *The Powwow Highway*. Rapid City, SD: Sky and Sage Books, 1996.

Shakespeare, Tom. *The Sky People*. New York: Vantage, 1971.

Silberman, Robert. "Opening the Text: *Love Medicine* and the Return of the Native
    American Woman." *Narrative Chance: Postmodern Discourses on Native Amer-
    ican Literatures*. Ed. Gerald Vizenor. Albuquerque: University of New Mex-
    ico Press, 1989. 101–20.

Silko, Leslie Marmon. *Ceremony*. New York: Penguin Books, 1977.

Smith, Gary. "Shadow of a Nation." *Sports Illustrated* 18 Feb. 1991. Rpt. *The Best
    American Sports Writing 1992*. Ed. Thomas McGhane. Boston: Houghton
    Mifflin Company, 1992. 1–23.

———. "Special Report." *Native Peoples* 15.6 (Sept./Oct. 2002): 26–27.

"Spirituality and the Sun Dance." 1 June 1998 <http://uts.cc.utexas.edu/~awk/
    blackfoot.htm>.

Stookey, Lorena. *Louise Erdrich: A Critical Companion*. Westport, CT: Greenwood
    Press, 1999.

Taylor, Colin. *North American Indians*. Bristol, Great Britain: Parragon, 1997.

Thornton, Russell J. *American Indian Holocaust and Survival: A Population History
    Since 1492*. Norman: University of Oklahoma Press, 1990.

Versluis, Arthur. *The Elements of Native American Traditions*. 1993. Shaftesbury, En-
    gland: Element, 1999.

Vizenor, Gerald, ed. *Narrative Chance: Postmodern Discourses on Native American
    Literatures*. Albuquerque: University of New Mexico Press, 1989.

Viola, Herman J. *Little Bighorn Remembered*. New York: Rivilo Books, 1999.

Wissler, Clark, and D. C. Duvall. *Mythology of the Blackfoot Indians*. 1908. Lincoln:
    University of Nebraska Press, 1995.

Wittstock, Laura Waterman, and Elaine J. Salinas. "A Brief History of the American Indian Movement." 2 Apr. 2003 <htttp://www.aimovement.org/ggc/history.html>.

Womack, Craig S. *Red on Red: Native American Literary Separatism*. Minneapolis: University of Minnesota Press, 1999.

Woodhead, Henry, ed. *The Reservations*. Alexandria, VA: Time-Life Books, 1995.

## Literature and Film Theory

Abrams, M. H. *A Glossary of Literary Terms*. 7th ed. New York: Harcourt, 1999.

Barry, Peter. *Beginning Theory*. 2nd ed. Manchester, England: Manchester University Press, 2002.

Bodkin, Maud. *Archetypal Patterns in Poetry*. 1934. New York: Vintage Books, 1961.

Bressler, Charles E. *Literary Criticism*. 3rd ed. Upper Saddle River, NJ: Prentice Hall, 2003.

Campbell, Joseph. *The Hero with a Thousand Faces*. New York: Meridian Books, 1956.

———. *The Power of Myth*. New York: Anchor Books, 1991.

*The Concise Columbia Encyclopedia*. Ed. Judith S. Levey and Agnes Greenhall. New York: Columbia University Press, 1983.

Evans, Mary. "Feminism before Psychoanalysis." *Feminism and Psychoanalysis: A Critical Dictionary*. Ed. Elizabeth Wright. Oxford: Blackwell Publishers, 1992. 98–103.

Ferguson, Margaret, Mary Jo Salter, and Jon Stallworthy, eds. *The Norton Anthology of Poetry*. 4th ed. New York: W. W. Norton, 1996.

Gibson, Donald B. "Richard Wright." *The Oxford Companion to African American Literature*. New York: Oxford University Press, 1997.

Groden, Michael, and Martin Kreiswirth, eds. *The Johns Hopkins Guide to Literary Theory and Criticism*. Baltimore: The Johns Hopkins University Press, 1994.

Harmon, William, and C. Hugh Holman. *A Handbook to Literature*. 8th ed. Upper Saddle River, NJ: Prentice Hall, 2000.

Hunter, Bob. "A Giant Stride for the Literature of Ecology." *Eye Weekly* 24 Sept. 1992. 12 Dec. 2002 <http://www.eye.net/eye/issue/issue/_09.24.92/NEWS/env0924.htm>.

Hurston, Zora Neale. "Characteristics of Negro Expression." 1934. *African American Literary Theory*. Ed. Winston Napier. New York: New York University Press, 2000. 31–44.

Iglesias, David Claudio. Review of *Windtalkers*. *Native Peoples* 15:5 (Jul./Aug. 2002): 90–93.

Jung, C. G. *Psychology and Religion*. New Haven, CT: Yale University Press, 1938.

Kaufmann, Walter. *Existentialism from Dostoevsky to Sartre*. 1956. New York: New American Library, 1975.

Kasdan, Margo, and Susan Tavernetti. "Native Americans in a Revisionist Western." In *Hollywood's Indian*. Ed. Peter Rollins and John E. O'Connor. Lexington: The University Press of Kentucky, 1998. 121–36.

Kilpatrick, Jacquelyn. *Celluloid Indians: Native Americans and Film*. Lincoln: University of Nebraska Press, 1999.

Kunuk, Zacharias. "The Art of Inuit Storytelling." *American Indian* 2.3 (Spring 2002): 34.

Lupton, Mary Jane. *Maya Angelou: A Critical Companion*. Westport, CT: Greenwood Press, 1998.

Lynn, Steven. *Texts and Contexts*. 2nd ed. New York: Addison Wesley Longman, 1998.

Majher, Jennifer. "The History and Theory of Magical Realism." 30 Jan. 2001 <http://www.southern.ohiou.edu/realmagic/JenniferM1.html>.

McKusick, James C. *Green Writing: Romanticism and Ecology*. New York: St. Martin's Press, 2000.

Monaghan, Peter. "Hot Type." *The Chronicle of Higher Education* 17 Jan. 2003: A16.

Murfin, Ross C. "Marxist Criticism and *Wuthering Heights*." *Wuthering Heights*. Ed. Linda H. Peterson. 2nd ed. Boston: Bedford/St. Martin's, 2003. 379–94.

Murfin, Ross, and Supryia M. Ray. *The Bedford Glossary of Critical and Literary Terms*. Boston: Bedford Books, 1997.

Niatum, Duane, ed. *Harper's Anthology of 20th Century Native American Poetry*. San Francisco: HarperCollins Publishers, 1988.

Noel, Natalie. "From *Windtalker* to *Skinwalker*." *Native Peoples* 15.6 (Sept./Oct. 2002): 41–44.

Rank, Otto. *The Myth of the Birth of the Hero*. 1952. New York: Robert Brunner, 1957.

Redshirt, Delphine. "A Conversation with Chris Eyre." *Native Peoples* 15:3 (Mar./Apr. 2002): 24–25.

Rogers, Bruce Holland. "What Is Magical Realism, Really?" *Speculations*. 23 Feb. 2003 <http://www.writing-world.com/sf/realism.html>.

Rollins, Peter, and John E. O'Connor, eds. *Hollywood's Indian*. Lexington: University Press of Kentucky, 1998.

Scott, A. O. "A Masterpiece. An Extraordinary Film." Rev. of *Atanarjuat: The Fast Runner*. *The New York Times* 30 Mar. 2002: Lot 47.com.

Selden, Raman. *A Reader's Guide to Contemporary Literary Theory*. 2nd ed. Lexington: University Press of Kentucky, 1989.

*Webster's New International Dictionary of the English Language*. 2nd ed. unabridged. Springfield, MA: C. and G. Merriam Company, 1949.

*Webster's New World Dictionary*. 2nd college ed. Ed. David B. Guralnik. New York: William Collins and the World Publishing Company, 1976.

## Non-Indian Writers

Achebe, Chinua. *Things Fall Apart*. 1968. Westport, CT: Heinemann, 1995.

Angelou, Maya. *A Song Flung up to Heaven*. New York: Random House, 2002.

Braly, Malcolm. *False Starts*. New York: Penguin Books, 1977.

———. *On the Yard*. 1967. New York: New York Review of Books, 2002.

158                              Bibliography

Bronte, Charlotte. *Jane Eyre*. 1847. Ed. Michael Mason. New York: Penguin Books, 1996.

Camus, Albert. *The Stranger*. 1942. Trans. Matthew Ward. New York: Vintage Books, 1988.

Cather, Willa Silbert. *Death Comes for the Archbishop*. 1927. New York: Vintage Books, 1990.

Cleaver, Eldridge. *Soul on Ice*. Introduction by Maxwell Grismar. New York: McGraw-Hill, 1968.

Charriere, Henri. *Papillon*. New York: Perennial, 2001.

Davis, Angela. *Angela Davis*. New York: Random House, 1974.

Dickens, Charles. *A Tale of Two Cities*. 1859. New York: Signet, 1997.

Ellison, Ralph. *Ralph Ellison's The Invisible Man*. Ed. Harold Bloom. 1952. New York: Chelsea House Publishers, 1996.

Fitzgerald, F. Scott. *The Great Gatsby. Three Great American Novels*. Introduction by Malcolm Cowley. New York: Charles Scribner's Sons, 1967.

Foucault, Michel. *Discipline and Punish: The Birth of the Prison*. Trans. by Alan Sheridan. New York: Vintage, 1995.

Gaddis, Thomas E. *Birdman of Alcatraz*. Mattituck, NY: Amereon, 1955.

Hemingway, Ernest. *In Our Time*. 1925. New York: Charles Scribner's Sons, 1986.

——. *The Sun Also Rises*. 1926. New York: Charles Scribner's Sons, 1956.

Homer. *The Odyssey. The Norton Anthology of World Masterpieces*. vol. 1. Ed. Maynard Mack. New York: W. W. Norton, 1995.

Jackson, George. *Soledad Brother*. 1970. Westport, CT: Lawrence Hill & Company, 1994.

King, Stephen. *The Shawshank Redemption*. New York: New American Library, 1994.

Kingston, Maxine Hong. *The Woman Warrior*. 1975. New York: Vintage, 1989.

Lowry, Malcolm. *Under the Volcano*. 1974. New York: New American Library, 1984.

Mailer, Norman. *The Executioner's Song*. 1979. New York: Vintage, 1998.

Malcolm X. *The Autobiography of Malcolm X: With the Assistance of Alex Haley*. New York: Grove Press, 1965.

Miller, Arthur. *Death of a Salesman*. 1949. New York: Penguin, 1998.

Morrison, Toni. *Beloved*. New York: Alfred A. Knopf, 1987.

Shelley, Mary. *Frankenstein*. New York: Bantam Classics, 2003.

Sophocles. *Oedipus Rex*. New York: Dover Publications, 1991.

Stevens, Anthony. *Private Myths*. Cambridge, MA: Harvard University Press, 1995.

Twain, Mark. *The Adventures of Huckleberry Finn*. Ed. John D. Seelye. New York: Penguin, 1986.

Virgil. *The Aeneid*. New York: Vintage Books, 1990.

Voltaire. *Candide*. 1789. Electronic Literature Foundation (ELF), 1999. Site closed.

Wright, Richard. "The Man Who Lived Underground." 1942. *Black Voices*. Ed. Abraham Chapman. New York: Mentor, 1968.

——. *Richard Wright's Native Son*. Ed. Harold Bloom. 1940. New York: Chelsea House Publishers, 1996.

## RECOMMENDED FILMS AND VIDEO ON NATIVE AMERICAN ISSUES

*Atanarjuat: The Fast Runner*. Dir. Zacharias Kunuk. Igloolik: Isuma Productions, 2002.

*Billy Jack*. Dir. T. C. Frank. Warner Brothers, 1971.

*The Black Robe*. Dir. Bruce Beresford. MGM Video, 1991.

*Buffalo Bill and the Indians*. Dir. Robert Altman. Metro Goldwyn Mayer, 1976.

*Cheyenne Autumn*. Dir. John Ford. Ford-Smith Productions, 1964.

*Clear Cut*. Dir. Richard Bugiaski. Cinexus Capital Corporation, 1992.

*Dances with Wolves*. Dir. Kevin Costner. Metro Goldwyn Mayer, 1990.

*The Deer Hunter*. Dir. Michael Cimino. Universal Studios Home Video, 1978.

*A Good Day to Die*. Dir. David Greene. Vidmark Entertainment, 1995.

*Geronimo*. Dir. Walter Hill. Columbia Pictures, 1994.

*House Made of Dawn*. Dir. Richardson Morse. New Line Cinema and Firebird Productions, 1996.

*Incident in Oglala*. Dir. Michael Apted. Presented by Robert Redford. Miramax Films, 1991.

*The Indian Wars*. Dir. Theodore Wharton. Produced by William Cody, 1914.

*Lakota Woman*. Dir. Frank Pierson. Turner Pictures, 1994.

*Last Stand at Little Bighorn*. Dir. Paul Stekler. The American Experience. Script by James Welch and Paul Stekler. WGBH/Boston, 1992.

*Leaving Las Vegas*. Dir. Mike Figgis. MGM Pictures, 1995.

*Medicine River*. Dir. Stuart Margolin. United American Video Corporation, 1994.

*Paha Sapa: The Black Hills*. Dir. Mel Lawrence. Home Box Office: Mystic Fire Video, 1993.

*Pocahontas*. Dir. Eric Goldberg. Walt Disney, 1995.

*Powwow Highway*. Dir. Jonathan Wacks. Hand Made Films, 1989.

*They Died With Their Boots On*. Dir. Raoul Walsh. 1941. MGM Home Entertainment, 1997.

*Smoke Signals*. Dir. Chris Eyre. Screenplay by Sherman Alexie. Produced by Shadowcatcher Entertainment. Miramax Films, 1998.

*Squanto: A Warrior's Tale*. Dir. Xavier Koller. Walt Disney Home Video, 1994.

*The Searchers*. Dir. John Ford. Warner Brothers, 1956.

*Skinwalker*. Dir. Chris Eyre. PBS, 24 Nov. 2002.

*StageCoach*. Dir. John Ford. United Artists, 1939.

*Thunderheart*. Dir. Michael Apted. Columbia TriStar, 1992.

*Twin Peaks*. Dir. David Lynch. 8 Apr. 1990. <http://twinpeaks.de/>.

*War Party*. Dir. Franc Roddam. Hemdale Film Corporation, 1989.

*Windtalkers*. Dir. John Woo. MGM Pictures, 2002.

# Index

**About the Author**

MARY JANE LUPTON is Professor Emeritus at Morgan State University in Baltimore, where she taught Native American Literature, and African American Literature. She is the author of *Maya Angelou: A Critical Companion* (Greenwood 2001).